CONTENTS

INTRODUCTION

I learned my cooking skills on the fly and on the go. As a child, I was the go-to holiday pie maker for family parties. I wielded frying pans and managed hot ovens. I deboned my own chickens and learned just how much mustard to use in a glaze. I learned knife skills and measuring ratios. I learned to read recipes or just wing it with ingredients we had around the house.

I learned to take charge.

I learned, most of all, to be creative.

Now, as a stay-at-home dad for nearly nine years running, I've moved on from pies and become a master at everything from the easy weeknight meal to the lazy weekend family dinner, from the healthful after-soccer snack to the classroom party treat. But I know I was capable of cooking real dishes at, say, age 10, and I'm teaching my daughter that she can do it, too. Cooking your own meals at a young age teaches independence and responsibility and lets kids enjoy a sense of pride and accomplishment. What kid can't use those qualities?

But it doesn't just happen one day. It requires work and practice and help. Thankfully, I've had a lot of help along the way, picking up beloved casserole recipes from my mom, Teena, and inventive tips and tricks from my wife, Dana. I've learned the art of a good dessert from my mother-in-law, Marilyn, and how to make the absolute best barbecue from my father-in-law, Duane.

Above all, I've learned from my daughter, Emmeline, that working together in the kitchen can provide some of the best, most joyful memories in the world.

Cooking, for us, is indeed a whole family affair.

In *Dad's Book of Awesome Recipes*, I will impart all the tips and tricks and recipes and wisdom I've learned over the years in the trenches of parenthood and from my entire family of top-notch chefs. You'll find delicious egg dishes for breakfast, easy sandwiches for lunch, fun-to-make and fun-to-eat snacks made with fruits and veggies, and dinners that will have everyone asking for seconds. In all of the sections, I tried to provide a well-balanced mix of recipes to keep the intermediate or advanced chef happy (Arzak-style eggs anyone? Gnocchi?) and the beginning sous chef confident (Apple pie in a bag? Don't mind if I do!).

In addition to all our own favorite family recipes, I'm pleased and proud to introduce you to a few other dads who provided some recipes that have become staples in their own homes.

These guys? They're amazing. I met them through the tight-knit dad blogging community and we've become good friends. When I decided to write a cookbook, I knew immediately they had to be involved. You'll be glad they are.

From Whit Honea's astoundingly large sandwich to Jason Sperber's mouthwatering kale potatoes, from Doyin Richards's Boomin' Banana Bread to Chris Routly's perfect gnocchi, their recipes and insights into cooking with kids make this book so much better, and I am so grateful for their contributions. These are dads who have huge hearts, and amazing knife skills to boot. I'm thrilled to feature their family favorites and hope you'll be just as delighted as I was at their creativity and talent.

Just like their families and mine, you and your tribe can experience the warm, delightful feeling of gathering in the kitchen and creating a wonderful meal together. Usually, there's laughter, joy, a big mess, and, sometimes, a magical mistake that somehow makes things even better.

I hope that in making these recipes you, too, will find that feeling of joy together.

TEACHING YOUR KIDS TO COOK THE AWESOME WAY

At first glance, this is a family cookbook. But look closer and it's so much more. I promise. It's also a conduit between you and the next generation of cooks in your family. It's a guidebook, a map, a compass rose. Just like your kids will remember how you taught them to shoot free throws or multiply fractions, they'll remember that you showed them the fastest way to dice an onion, how to tell if an egg is cooked, and how to bake a mean cake.

This book should be used as an opportunity for passing on those important cooking skills to the next generation, for letting kids tinker in the kitchen, unleash creative sides, and learn, along the way, important life skills that will make them not just masters of the kitchen but masters of what they put in their bodies. Let's face it: There's a ton of junk available out there for very little money. Teaching kids to cook and use quality, healthful ingredients keeps them not just fed but healthy as well.

Let Your Kids Take the Lead

That's the main philosophy of this book.

In an age of bubble-wrapped childhoods and helicopter parenting, I want *Dad's Book of Awesome Recipes* to provide that old-school throwback vibe when kids were given looser reins and more responsibility.

In short, if there's any takeaway from this book, it's this: Let the kids take the lead.

Most kids already want to emulate their parents and do the same things they do. That's why toy companies make kid-friendly workbenches, doctor kits—and kitchens. So don't shoo them out of the real kitchen. Instead, invite them in.

You and me? We *know* how to make a grilled cheese sandwich. We're adults. We can make *all manner* of dishes. We can manage sizzling frying pans and hot ovens. We can handle knives and rolling pins and electric mixers.

But young chefs? They will delight in making something we consider incredibly easy. They will feel pride and joy and a happiness that will urge them on toward more complicated meals and fun times in the family kitchen. As an adult, you may think, "Fruit on a stick? That's *it*?" Believe me, I get it, I do. Some of these recipes may seem ridiculously simple to adults. But again, to a beginning chef working on a first recipe, it may well be a Michelin-starred culinary adventure. You have to start somewhere, and I hope kids and adults find a few fun recipes to start that journey together. You don't always have to go big. Sometimes you just have to go. So there are plenty of recipes in here for the littlest beginners.

If you've got an older child or an experienced chef, steer them toward forays into cooking the perfect steak . . . attempts at recreating simple lasagnas in individual "cup cakes" . . . and throwing together an easy, delicious side dish. (If you have an advanced chef, swap roles! *You* prep or wash and clean while he or she pulls everything together.)

Throughout the book, you'll notice there are many sections where I urge you to get your little sous chefs involved. This is really more of a reminder than anything. The *whole book* is designed for them to take the lead, with many of my favorite family recipes tailored for small hands and beginning chefs.

A Guidebook to Creativity

When it comes to some recipes, you have to follow the instructions closely. Add baking soda and powder to the mix and you have light and fluffy pancakes. Leave those ingredients out, and you have crepes. From cakes to flapjacks to cookies to fudge, there are plenty of recipes in here that can teach kids to follow directions, to measure, to be precise. These are indeed important skills. Pass them on.

But there are also scores of recipes in here designed to let kids unleash their creative sides. You'll notice I use lots of "pinches" of salt or "drizzles" of olive oil or "splashes" of hot sauce, rather than precise measurements. I want young chefs to learn not just how to follow a recipe but how to make it their own, how to make it sing, how to make it *better*.

I like to think that this book provides the canvas and paints, and they provide the unique painting.

So if there are recipes where they want to skip the salt, or maybe add an extra pinch instead, by all means, let them. If they feel the recipe for Sloppyish Joes requires more or less ketchup, it's their call. If they think the Agua Fresca needs more sugar or, say, a squeeze of lime, again, give them the go-ahead to see what happens.

I watch a lot of cooking shows and read a lot of cookbooks, and I greatly admire the way chef Jamie Oliver implores people to let their imaginations go wild. Rough chops, pinches, drizzles, mashing, mixing—he urges people to dig in and worry less about making everything perfect and pretty and instead focus on making it delicious and easy. That's pretty good advice and I've adopted it for our own family cooking adventures. I urge you to follow it as well. Get messy, use your hands, be creative. Have fun.

Kitchen Skills for Kids

This part always makes me feel like a lawyer. To be honest, the publisher makes me say this stuff. We far too often bubble-wrap childhood and don't let kids experience danger. Knives, stoves, toasters, mixers . . . yes, they can be dangerous. But they can also be incredibly useful, and unless you plan on cooking for your kids for the rest of your life, it's best they learn how to use them. Indeed, before you unleash your kids in the kitchen, make sure they know basic safety skills. Obviously, hot

food or pans, boiling water, and sharp knives can all cause injury—and your child's first trip to the ER is not the kind of family memory we're trying to make. But remember that you're trying to pass on some great life skills here and no one knows your own kids better than you. So go over these safety tips, impart any of your own, and get ready to hand over the reins if you think they're up to it.

- **Always hang around the kitchen while they're cooking.** Remember, they're still kids, and you need to be there if a potentially harmful situation arises. But mostly you should be there because cooking for the family is supposed to be a family event. Then again, if they're older and kitchen pros, kick back with some coffee and the newspaper. Again, nothing replaces your own judgment.

- **Wash hands!** Teach your kids that they should wash their hands with soap and water before touching food and again right after handling raw meat, chicken, or fish before they touch other things.

- **Tie back kids' long hair and roll up long sleeves.** First, you want to keep them out of the food. Second, for safety reasons you need to keep long or loose items away from things like blenders or the flame on the stove.

- **Read the entire recipe with your kids before you begin.** Show them how to assemble ingredients and utensils they will need.

- **Be sure you're starting with a clean cooking area.** Otherwise, dirty dishes will be in your way, dirty counters will ruin your food, and other things on the counter or table (such as mail) may get stained or splashed.

- **Always use potholders or oven mitts to touch hot pans and dishes.** You may not realize how hot something is until you've touched it or picked it up, so it's always better to start out with your hands protected.

- **Don't overfill pots and pans.** This is one thing that can easily lead to a dangerous situation. If pots overflow while you are cooking, you will at best end up with a mess and at worst might get splattered or burned with hot liquids.

- **Teach your kids exactly how to use the various appliances they will need.** Show them what each button and knob does, and how to turn them on and off. Keep electric appliances away from water or the sink. Keep the cords up on the counter so no one trips or steps on them by accident.

- **Teach proper knife usage.** They should be holding the knife and the food in a way that minimizes potential accidents. (Chop with one hand on the handle, for instance, while your other hand is flat and atop the blade, pressing down. This helps speed up chopping, while also keeping those pesky fingers out of the way of the sharp end of the knife.) If *you're* not 100 percent sure how, teach yourself then teach your kids. There are plenty of fantastic knife skills videos on YouTube nowadays and I watch them from time to time to gain new skills myself. Speaking of Jamie Oliver again . . . he has some great videos on YouTube. Watch a few and take the best tips you can get. (You'll also find some pretty cool videos on how to slice up kitchen favorites, such as mango or pomegranates. Definitely worth a watch.)

- **Do only one job at a time.** Cooking requires planning and concentration. So shut off the TV, leave the phones in the other room, and, especially in the beginning, just focus on the cooking.

- **Clean up!** Set a good example by putting ingredients away when you have finished with them. Also, be sure to wipe down, unplug, and turn off all appliances when you're done. Wipe counters clean while working. Put dirty dishes in the sink, then wash them.

These tips are important, but look, again, you know your kids better than anyone. You know if your 4-year-old is ready to wield a paring knife for slicing and dicing veggies. Or perhaps you think it's best to wait until he's, say, 27. Cool. Use your best judgment.

So if you think your older child is ready to make a pasta dish or cook a great steak, read the recipe together, provide a little coaching, and then step aside. If you think your beginning chef needs some lessons in knife work or other tools, work on the recipes together and make some great memories to go along with that amazing side dish.

Take Your Time

When it comes to whipping up a weekday meal on a busy evening, it's often easier for me to just head to the kitchen and slam a few ingredients together while my daughter finishes her homework and my wife commutes home.

But when I'm cooking with Emme, I try my best to remember to take it slow. Things will usually take a little longer. If I don't remember this, I tend to get antsy and sometimes grumpy or hangry (hungry + angry), to be honest.

But if I go in knowing we're going to make a fun meal together and it's going to take a bit longer than it'd take me to do it alone, there is magic in the house. It's a warm feeling. There's laughter and fun and bonding. I wouldn't trade that feeling for the world.

How Much Time Will I Need?

With some of the simpler recipes in this book, you still won't need much time. But if you're working with a first-timer or if your advanced chef is taking on something particularly challenging, remember to be patient.

Unlike a lot of recipe books, I decided not to put a time estimate for preparation and cooking. Instead, I graded them based on "Easy," "Medium," or "Hard."

Here's why: I really didn't want parents or beginning chefs to feel discouraged that their 10-minute side dish actually took 45 minutes. When they grow up or gain serious skills later on (something I hope this book helps with), they can whip up recipes in an estimated time frame. But

for now, it's about learning and cooking together and having fun—and there should be no time limits on that.

(Fine, fine, if you absolutely *must* know, I'd put most "Easy" recipes in the 10–15 minute range. But again, it depends on how much you let your child do and how advanced he is with, say, a chef's knife. Medium recipes will probably take 20–30 minutes. Hard recipes will obviously take the longest, 30 minutes or more . . . at least in the beginning. Take the DIY Arzak-ish Eggs, for instance. It took me a half hour when I first tried it. Now, it usually takes 10 minutes, tops. There's still a lot of skill and perfect timing involved, but as they say, practice makes perfect.)

Trust Me: It's Worth the Wait

There's a terrific benefit to taking your time and going slow and letting kids really get their hands dirty: They learn to do it themselves. When Emme first started helping out with recipes, it took a long, long time for her to measure out amounts of flour or salt or milk. There were mistakes and remeasurements.

Now, I can just plop a recipe in front of her, and she gathers all the ingredients and measures everything out just perfectly. This comes from giving her the freedom to practice from an early age, from teaching skills and letting her run with them. Yes, it takes time. But it will happen.

The teamwork and kitchen camaraderie is a true joy in my life and working in the kitchen as a family is one of the things I'm most grateful for.

I hope, above all else, that cooking the recipes in this book gives you that feeling too.

BREAKFAST

2

When it comes to breakfast, I'm torn. On weekend days, I enjoy the long, luxurious diner experience: the flapjacks and bacon, the hot coffee and scrambled eggs. On busy weekday mornings, sometimes stuffing my face with a bowl of oatmeal is the best I can do.

In this section, you're going to find recipes for both types of mornings. Together with your mini chef, you're going to create the most delicious, buttery Dutch Baby you've ever had for that lazy weekend morning. But you're also going to toss together simple eggs and toast dishes for crazy schoolday mornings.

In the end, breakfast is far, far too important to get out of a box 365 days a year. With these recipes at your disposal, you and your chef are going to make light work of any breakfast dish—whether you're hurriedly trying to get out the door or just hanging around for too long in your PJs.

FRUIT AND MINT SKEWERS

DIFFICULTY: Easy • **MAKES:** 6 skewers

I'm not a big fan of hiding good, healthy food behind something else. Instead, I like to prepare the good, healthy food in fun, flavorful ways and then present it over and over again as part of a balanced meal. Sometimes the kid eats it; sometimes not. But it's there and it's delicious and that's just how I roll. Fruit and Mint Skewers are an awesome, easy way to get kids excited about healthy food. They're fun to eat, taste great, and are simple enough for kids to whip up by themselves in a flash. Yes, threading fruit on a stick is easy for you and me. But kids always enjoy a sense of accomplishment after doing this, and the fun of eating stuff off skewers will have them stuffing their faces with healthy food in no time.

Here's what you need:

TOOLS
❑ Knife, cutting board, bowl, toothpicks or longer skewers

INGREDIENTS
❑ Fruit of choice (cantaloupe, mango, orange, and honeydew go well with mint, but use what you have)

❑ Small bunch of fresh mint

Here's what you do:

1 I'm going to use cantaloupe. You can use anything you have or like, but I like cantaloupe and this is my book, so there. Slice the cantaloupe into bite-sized squares. They don't have to be perfect. Let your sous chef do this part if she's ready. Add the fruit to a bowl.

2 Group and wash a whole mess of mint and give it a rough chop. Again, don't worry about making perfect, uniform pieces. Let the kids take the lead if they're up for it.

3 Add the mint to the bowl and stir.

4 Now slide the fruit onto your toothpicks or skewers until you have 4 or 5 chunks on each skewer, or however many you prefer.

BLENDER JUICE

DIFFICULTY: Easy • **MAKES:** 2 tall glasses

A delicious, healthy drink . . . what's not to love? This is a go-to favorite for getting a side of fruit into breakfast with very, very little (if any) added sugar. In fact, I just add a pinch to give the appearance of sweetness, but depending on the ripeness of the fruit you're using, you might just skip it. This recipe is sort of like an agua fresca but with less sugar, so use any fruit you have or particularly like. This one uses mango, our favorite.

Here's what you need:

TOOLS

❏ Knife, cutting board, blender, glasses

INGREDIENTS

❏ 1 large mango

❏ Approximately 1 cup water

❏ 1 pinch sugar (optional)

❏ 1 sprig mint or basil (optional)

❏ Some ice

Here's what you do:

1 Slice and dice your mango. Now, there are special ways to cut a mango (hedgehog style, for instance). But you're going to throw everything into the blender anyway and grind it all up, so don't worry how your sous chef decides to cut it. Just help her cut the long pit out of the middle and then she can make chunks.

2 Add chunks to blender with your water, starting with about ½ cup water and adding more if needed. Add a pinch of sugar or mint if you like or if you think the mango needs it.

3 Blend into oblivion—about 30 to 45 seconds.

4 Pour into large glass. You can spoon off the foam if you like, or just let it settle. Add some ice to cool everything down. Yum. Mmmm. Gulp.

SIMPLE FRIED EGG

DIFFICULTY: Easy-medium • **MAKES:** 1 ridiculously good fried egg

A good fried egg is warm, salty, yolky, and hits that umami spot in the secret pleasure zones of your mouth. But the best part is just how easy it is for anyone to make. You're cracking an egg into a hot pan and then performing a tiny touch of magic to get it just right. Add some toast or, even better, *buttered toast sticks*, and your little sous chef is going to have a great breakfast meal she can do all on her own in no time at all.

Here's what you need:

TOOLS

❏ Stove, frying pan, lid to cover pan, spatula, spoon

INGREDIENTS

❏ 1 tablespoon butter

❏ 1 egg

❏ 1 teaspoon water

❏ Pinches of salt and pepper to taste, (optional)

❏ Buttered toast sticks, (optional)

Here's what you do:

1 Preheat your pan on the stove at medium heat while you assemble your ingredients.

2 Add butter to pan and use spatula to coat all areas. Your mouth should be watering at this point.

3 Crack your egg into the pan so that the yolk remains intact.

4 Now here's the fun part: Add a spoonful of water around the egg and then put the lid on so that it covers the pan. Here's what happens: The pan fries the egg just so on the bottom, but the water turns to steam and cooks the top of the egg so much better than doing it lidless. No need to attempt a messy flip.

5 After a minute, lift the lid and check it out. If the egg white appears runny, cook a little longer. If it looks firm and just moist, it's ready. Of course, taste is all up to your chef. If she likes a well-done yolk, keep cooking. But a good minute or so should give you a firmish egg white with a warm yolk that will ooze when poked.

6 If you think it's ready, gently and confidently slide your spatula underneath the whole egg. You don't have to do it in one fell swoop. Push in a little at a time, pulling the spatula back and forth until it's all the way under the egg. Don't stress if the yolk breaks or the egg falls apart. It takes a bit to get it right, but that's where practice comes into play. Have fun and enjoy the accomplishment of making family food together.

7 Plate your egg and sprinkle with salt and pepper if you like. My daughter loves to dip buttered toast sticks into the yolk, but let your own child call the shots.

DAD TIP

If your children need practice cracking eggs over something less stressful than a hot stove, try cracking the egg into a bowl first. That way, you can remove any shells that might accidentally slip in. Then slowly slide the egg from the bowl into the frying pan.

SOFT-BOILED EGG AND TOAST SOLDIERS

DIFFICULTY: Medium • **MAKES:** 1 egg and 1 slice of toast

We're a family in love with eggs. And soft-boiling them is probably one of our favorite ways to showcase all the magic you can do with them. After a quick bath and a little top-chopping, these guys become creamy and dense and just short of heavenly. Dip in a few slender, salty toast sticks, and you've got a fun, nutritious, and mind-blowing breakfast that really doesn't take that long or require much more than a pot of water and a toaster.

Here's what you need:

TOOLS
❏ Stove, pot, big spoon, toaster, clean dishtowel, knife

INGREDIENTS
❏ 1 egg

❏ 1 slice bread

❏ 1 tablespoon butter

❏ Salt and pepper to taste

Here's what you do:

1 Add water to your pot. You probably don't need a *ton* of water, because, come on, eggs are small. Just use enough water to cover the egg by an inch or so and bring to a boil.

2 Once the water is boiling, spoon in your egg. I say spoon in, because you don't want to just throw a raw egg into a metal pot. It could crack. Not good. So place an egg on a spoon and gently lower it into the water until the egg hits the bottom. If your sous chef has confident hands, let her do it.

3 Now here's the tricky part: timing. Boil the egg for exactly 4 minutes and 30 seconds; that seems to be the perfect sweet spot for soft-boiled eggs. (I guess it also depends on the egg. If it is super jumbo extra large, an extra few seconds in the hot bath would be a good idea.)

4 As your eggs are boiling under the timer, it's time to make your toast. Plop the bread in the toaster and get your butter and salt and pepper ready.

5 While keeping an eye on your egg timer, take out your finished toast and butter it before cutting it into strips or sticks.

6 Then head over to the pot. When the timer is up, spoon the egg out and place on a clean towel draped over a cutting board. (Drain the hot water in the sink.) You can even run the egg very quickly under cold water to make it easier to handle. The egg is going to be hot or warm at this point, but holding it for a few seconds at a time with moving fingers won't kill you.

7 Once the egg is ready, use your knife to gently crack a circle around the top—about half an inch down. Just tap tap tap the knife around the entire top.

8 Now, with the same knife, quickly chop off the top of the egg. Be confident. Use a steady, sure hand, and press down quickly and firmly. You're basically decapitating the egg, so don't make it suffer or the yolk will spill out.

9 Once you cut the top off, you can serve in any fashion you like—in an egg dish, in a bowl, in a small mug. Just make sure the egg stands upright. Add your toast sticks to the dish or on the side and sprinkle some salt and pepper around the sticks and egg top. Then just start dipping the toast sticks and using a spoon to eat the egg right out of the shell.

PERFECT POPOVERS

DIFFICULTY: Easy • **MAKES:** 6 popovers

Popovers are sort of like pancake muffins. Warm, golden brown, and just sweet enough with a side of syrup. They're perfect for packing breakfast on the go or for a lazy weekend morning treat. They're also an easy breakfast recipe that requires just a bowl, some measuring utensils, and a whisk. You can make them in a popover pan, a muffin pan, or even small custard cups. However you make them, you're in for a treat.

Here's what you need:

TOOLS

❑ Oven, muffin pan, oven mitts, large bowl, whisk, measuring cups and spoons

INGREDIENTS

❑ Cooking oil spray

❑ 3 eggs

❑ 1 cup milk

❑ 1 cup all-purpose flour

❑ 3 tablespoons butter, melted

❑ Dash of salt

Here's what you do:

1 Preheat the oven to 375°F and spray your muffin pan with cooking spray.

2 Crack all your eggs in a large bowl and give them a good whisking. This could be nice practice for any little ones who are new to egg cracking.

3 Next, add the milk, flour, melted butter, and a dash of salt and whisk it all together until it's nice and smooth—no lumps.

4 Now it's time to cook. Pour the batter into the muffin pan so each cup is about ⅔ full. They'll puff up, so be careful not to fill too high.

5 Now bake for 25–35 minutes until they're golden brown. Insert a knife or toothpick into one to test. If the knife is wet with dough, keep cooking. If it comes out clean, you're ready to eat. Only test one, however, so you don't deflate the others.

6 Use your mitts to remove the pan and then gently tap the popovers free onto a plate (use a knife to pry them out if they don't fall out on their own). We like to serve them with jam or butter or drizzle them with syrup, depending on the mood of the day. You really can't go wrong.

CINNAMON RAISIN FRENCH TOAST STICKS

DIFFICULTY: Medium • **MAKES:** About 24 sticks

With this recipe, you're going to make traditional French toast using cinnamon raisin bread (or really any thick bread you enjoy and think will make for a delicious breakfast treat). When you're finished cooking the toast, you're going to flop it on a cutting board and cut the pieces into long sticks. Seriously, that's it. Just a few slices and dices and suddenly an average breakfast is transformed into something kids can't resist. I don't know why, but simply cutting stuff into sticks makes lots of things easier and more fun to eat.

Here's what you need:

TOOLS

❑ Stove, frying pan or griddle, measuring cup and spoons, pie plate, whisk, zester, spatula, knife, cutting board

INGREDIENTS

❑ 3 eggs

❑ ½ cup milk

❑ 1 orange to zest

❑ 2 tablespoons butter, divided

❑ 8 slices cinnamon raisin bread

❑ Syrup and powdered sugar for finishing and serving

Here's what you do:

1 First things first: You need to make a bath for your toast. Whisk the eggs and milk in the pie plate until well mixed. I like to zest in some orange peel. It adds a nice touch of holiday flavor, but you can skip it if that's not your thing or you don't enjoy holidays and flavor.

2 Now your bath is ready. If your bread is super thick, add a couple of slices and let them soak. If it's thinner, move on to the next part first before dunking the bread. (Some breads just don't need a long soak, while others do. Use your judgment.) After all, the next part is easy: Melt 1 tablespoon of butter in your frying pan over medium-high heat.

3 So now your frying pan is ready to go and you're ready to cook. Remove your bread slices from the bath and grill as many as you can at a time. Cook about 1 to 2 minutes per side until each side is golden brown. When finished with your first slices, melt the other tablespoon of butter on the frying pan, dunk some more bread into the bath, and then grill those as well.

4 When you're finished with the whole batch, move the toast to a cutting board and slice up into as many sticks as you please (I got the serving size by cutting 8 slices of bread into 4 sticks each). Thin, thick, small, large . . . let your sous chef decide.

5 Move the sticks to a plate and sprinkle a dash of sugar on top and serve with a small cup of syrup to dunk into.

DAD TIP

You can use just about any bread you like or have on hand. I like the cinnamon bread without raisins myself, but kids seem to like raisins, so there you go. If you have regular white or wheat bread and don't feel like running to the store, that works just fine. Add some cinnamon and orange zest to the bath and voila! You're good to go.

EASY MORNING CREPES

DIFFICULTY: Medium, bordering on hard because of flip • **MAKES:** 6 to 8 crepes

I've had crepes all over Paris. In nice restaurants, hotels, and street vendors under the Eiffel Tower. But nothing compares to my mother-in-law's crepes. They're thin and sweet with just the right amount of dough feel in the mouth. Add some strawberries and sweet cream, or spritz with lemon and sprinkles of sugar, and you just can't go wrong. What I like about making them my mother-in-law's way is that you don't have to stress over size. A true crepe is cooked on an enormous round griddle about the size of a small bike tire. The batter is spread thin and then just try flipping that enormous thing. Doing it yourself in a large frying pan at home means you can control the size and get it just right for you. It'll probably take you a few times to get the flip just right, but once you do . . . food heaven. *Ooh la la.*

Here's what you need:

TOOLS

❑ Stove, large frying pan, large mixing bowl, measuring cups and spoons, whisk, spatula

INGREDIENTS

❑ 3 eggs

❑ 1½ cups milk

❑ 4 tablespoons butter, divided

❑ 1 tablespoon granulated sugar

❑ ½ teaspoon salt

❑ 1 cup all-purpose flour

❑ Some lemon wedges

❑ 1 tablespoon powdered sugar

❑ Syrup or fruit for filling (optional)

Here's what you do:

1 Beat the eggs in a large bowl.

2 Add milk, 2 tablespoons melted butter, granulated sugar, and salt and whisk well.

3 Now add flour and mix again. You want a nice, thin, smooth batter.

4 In a large frying pan, melt about a tablespoon of butter over medium-high heat. Use the spatula to coat the sides and bottom of pan.

5 Pour about ½ cup of the batter into the pan and then tilt pan until batter covers entire surface. You want it to be big. Cook until golden brown on bottom and tiny bubbles appear on top, approximately 1 minute.

6 Now here's the fun part: flipping. Think of it as a big pancake. The only thing is, when you're cooking a pancake, you can usually just jam the spatula under the whole thing and flip it. Easy. The crepe, however, is big and tricky. It's difficult to get the spatula under the whole thing. Ahh but remember: You are the boss. You can start by making smaller crepes to get a handle on it first. Or you can just go bigtime right away. Either way, don't let your little kid stress. It's tricky for everyone and not all crepes will be perfect. Use your spatula to lift up an entire side and then go ahead and use your fingers to help flip it over. It'll be warm but it's so thin that the air will cool the part you raised.

7 Cook for another 30 to 45 seconds—it doesn't need much—and then you can spatula it out of the frying pan or sort of slide it out by gripping the frying pan handle and tilting it while shaking. The crepe should begin to slide. Use a spatula to help.

8 Once you have a few on a plate ready to go, simply grab one and roll it up. Spritz it with lemon and sprinkle with dashes of powdered sugar. If you'd like, add berries and then roll up. Either way, you're in for something special.

SWEET CANDY BACON

DIFFICULTY: Easy peasy • **MAKES:** 6 strips

I know what you're thinking: It's bacon. How can it get any better? Well, it can. Oh, it can. The best part, beyond the deliciousness, is how easy it is for kids to make something that will literally bring "oohs and ahhs" from anyone who eats it. That's got to make a beginner chef proud and happy. Just thinking about these makes my mouth water, so let's get right to it.

Here's what you need:

TOOLS

❑ Oven, baking pan, 2 or 3 cooling racks, oven mitts, small bowl, sauce brush

INGREDIENTS

❑ 6 strips bacon, the thicker the better

❑ ¼ cup maple syrup

Here's what you do:

1 Preheat the oven to 400°F. If you have a convection roasting feature, use that. If not, regular baking will work fine.

2 While the oven is warming, grab your cooling racks and place them inside the baking pan. There should be about ¼" of space between the pan and the cooling racks. This allows hot oven air to get under the bacon and cook all over.

3 Lay your bacon strips atop the cooling racks so that the strips run perpendicular to the rack rods.

4 Now paint! Pour syrup into a small bowl and then dip your brush and paint each strip. Then set aside syrup. Seriously, this whole process should be done by your child. Nothing is hot yet. It's just bacon laying and painting. Any kid can do it.

Yes, there will be syrup everywhere and your kid will probably smell like some combination of raw pork and syrup but, well, yeah. Given the raw meat situation, I should probably advise you to be sure he washes his hands thoroughly afterward. But don't stress. Think of the powerful immune system you're building. See? Bacon really *is* the best.

5 When your oven is ready, put the bacon in. Cook for about 10 minutes.

6 After 10 minutes, pull pan out and place on another cooling rack. Being careful not to touch pan, paint another coat of syrup on the bacon and then put back in the oven.

7 Cook for another 1 to 2 minutes, or until it's done to your desired crispiness level. I like almost well-done bacon with a hint of meaty chewiness, while my wife and daughter prefer well done and crispy. Remove, plate, then listen for gasps of sugar bacon pleasure.

POWER GRANOLA

DIFFICULTY: Medium   •   **MAKES:** 3 cups

The great thing about granola is how healthy it can be. The bad thing about granola is how *unhealthy* it can be. On one hand, homemade granola is just loaded with good food: seeds, nuts, oats, dried fruit. It's a nutritional and good-fat powerhouse that also happens to taste great. On the other hand, commercial granola is usually just as loaded with endless amounts of sugar. I like making it at home because you can make a delicious, healthy snack or breakfast cereal while controlling the amount of sugar and the ingredients. Although it makes for a great day starter, you can also bag it for a pre-sport snack.

Here's what you need:

TOOLS

❑ Oven, baking pan, oven mitts, measuring cups and spoons, large bowl, small bowl, large spoons, cooking spoon

INGREDIENTS

❑ 1½ cups rolled oats (not instant)

❑ ½ cup shelled sunflower seeds

❑ ¼ cup pumpkin seeds

❑ ¼ cup flax seeds (optional)

❑ ½ cup chopped almonds

❑ ½ cup dried cranberries (or raisins, blueberries, raspberries, you name it . . . but avoid anything coated in sugar)

❑ 2 tablespoons melted butter

❑ 1 tablespoon canola oil

❑ 1 tablespoon honey

❑ 1 tablespoon molasses

Here's what you do:

1 Preheat oven to 375°F.

2 In a large bowl, combine grains, seeds, nuts, and dried fruit.

3 In a small bowl, combine all your liquids—butter, oil, honey, and molasses.

4 Now the fun! Pour liquid over nuts and then mix around into a slurry of coated granola. Almost there. Be sure to let the kids do all this while you sip coffee and enjoy not getting so sticky.

5 Now spread your sticky granola onto baking pan into an even layer. No enormous clumps. But again, enjoy that coffee and let the kids figure it out.

6 Put it into the oven and bake for 10 minutes. While it's cooking, reach in and stir around with cooking spoon once or twice to keep spots from burning. Be careful, obviously.

7 Remove, stir a bit, and let cool. When it's good and cool, store in an airtight container.

TRADITIONAL EGG IN TOAST

DIFFICULTY: Medium • **MAKES:** 1 egg in toast

Some dishes just put a smile on kids' faces, and this is surely one of them. There's something about taking the ordinary—bread—and doing something special with it—tossing in a cooked egg. The toast is buttery and crunchy, and the egg becomes a nice "dipping pool." Definitely a breakfast favorite.

Here's what you need:

TOOLS

❑ Stove, large frying pan, cookie cutter or small drinking glass, spatula

INGREDIENTS

❑ 1 slice bread

❑ 1 tablespoon butter, divided

❑ 1 egg

❑ Salt and pepper to taste

Here's what you do:

1 Warm up the frying pan over low-medium heat.

2 Cut a hole out of the bread by using a circular cookie cutter or the rim of a small drinking glass. Just set in middle and press down until you have a round hole. This is where the egg will go.

3 Place ½ tablespoon butter in pan and add bread. Quickly crack egg into hole and let egg cook for about 3 minutes. Place round toast you cut out next to bread in the pan for toasting.

4 When egg firms up, do your very best to slide spatula underneath without breaking yolk. It takes practice. Don't let kids get too frustrated at first—it's a skill.

5 Add remaining ½ tablespoon butter to pan while bread is lifted up on spatula and then flip bread gently into pan. Cook for another minute or so, depending on how done the kids like the egg. The shorter you cook it, the yolkier it will be. Don't forget to flip the round toast as well!

6 Remove from pan, sprinkle with salt and pepper, and serve with the round toast as the dunkee for your new egg-in-toast swimming hole.

RAINBOW PANCAKES

DIFFICULTY: Medium • **MAKES:** 1 dozen cakes

You may want to make this recipe by yourself at first. Keep the kids out of the kitchen altogether. After they see the big reveal, they can help next time. But this time . . . I vote that you give it a try yourself and watch the incredible smile of joy spread across their faces as you plop down a stack of steaming pancakes. But not just any pancakes. *Rainbow pancakes*. I promise oohs and ahhs. Then you can teach them the trick the next morning. Win. Win.

Here's what you need:

TOOLS

❏ Stove, oven, large frying pan or griddle pan, oven mitts, measuring cups and spoons, large mixing bowl, lots of small mixing bowls, lots of spoons, whisk, spatula

INGREDIENTS

❏ 1 cup all-purpose flour

❏ 1 tablespoon sugar

❏ 1½ teaspoons baking powder

❏ ½ teaspoon baking soda

❏ Pinch salt

❏ 1 egg

❏ 1½ cups buttermilk

❏ 1 tablespoon butter, melted

❏ 1 tablespoon butter, not melted

❏ Food coloring (preferably all the colors of the rainbow, but even 4 does the job just fine)

❏ Syrup

Here's what you do:

1 In a large bowl, combine the flour, sugar, baking powder, baking soda, and a pinch of salt.

2 Lightly beat an egg in a separate bowl. Then add egg, buttermilk, and melted butter to your flour mix. Whisk until smooth.

3 Now, divide batter into as many small bowls as you have separate colors for. Pretty easy, really. Just pour, and then add a few drops of food coloring until the mix is bright. (They tend to mute themselves during cooking, but don't worry about it. They'll still be plenty colorful with only a few drops.)

4 Now heat your pan on low heat and butter it up.

5 Make a batch of, say, blue first. And then green. And then red, and yellow. Stick with one color at a time, so they don't blend on the griddle. Cook until light brownish on the edges and then flip.

6 As you finish each batch, plop them onto an oven-safe plate and stick the plate into a warm oven (200°F or less) to keep them ready for eating while you finish all the colors.

7 Plate all the colored pancakes and get ready to serve. Have everything ready when the kids come in. Maybe even sit them down with their eyes closed, then plop the plate down in front of them. Serve with syrups, oohs, and ahhs.

CINNAMON LEFTOVER RICE PUDDING

DIFFICULTY: Easy • **MAKES:** 1 bowl

Have you ever opened the fridge in the morning for breakfast and noticed a carton of leftover white rice from last night's dinner? Sometimes it gets a little hard and just feels . . . not right. I'm not saying it's unsafe to eat. You're just not sure whether to toss it or keep it. Well, *keep* it. And then make this delicious rice pudding breakfast with it.

Here's what you need:

TOOLS

❑ Microwave, measuring cups, serving bowl, stirring spoon, towel or oven mitts

INGREDIENTS

❑ ½ cup rice

❑ ¼–½ cup milk

❑ Cinnamon to taste

❑ Sugar or honey to taste

Here's what you do:

1 Take your rice and dump it into a bowl. Seriously, this is something even the smallest of small cooks can do, so teach and then get out of the way.

2 Now add milk and stir. I like my pudding just on the border between runny and solid, so I tend to add more milk. Stir in as much as you like until it's the consistency you want.

3 Add the cinnamon and sugar to taste. I tend to bolster the spice but skimp on the sweet, as it's usually a breakfast food for us. Give it a taste or two until your child finds just the right combo for his taste buds. I wouldn't use more than a few teaspoons of sugar, otherwise it becomes a sugary soup.

4 Now toss in the microwave for 2 minutes. Be careful when removing the bowl, as it gets awfully hot sometimes. Use a towel or oven mitts and then let it cool a little bit.

DAD TIP

Use a fork to break up the rice after you add milk for a smoother, more pudding-like consistency, or let soak for a few minutes before or after heating.

SPICY BREAKFAST TACO

DIFFICULTY: Medium • **MAKES:** 1 taco

For the longest time I shied away from spicy food for breakfast. But on family trips to the farmers' market in the San Francisco Ferry Building, my wife Dana and daughter Emme would gobble up plate after plate of spicy Mexican egg dishes from our favorite breakfast stand. Emme was 3 or so at the time, and I figured if she could do it, then so could I. I followed her lead and was astonished at how wonderful it was to start your day with a little kick. If your kids like dinner tacos, try this breakfast version on a hurried weekday.

Here's what you need:

TOOLS

❑ Stove, frying pan, measuring cups and spoons, small mixing bowls, fork, cheese grater, stirring spoon, knife, cutting board

INGREDIENTS

❑ ½ tablespoon butter or cooking spray

❑ 1 egg

❑ Queso fresco or any cheese you like, to grate into ¼ cup

❑ 1 tortilla

❑ ¼ cup diced tomato

❑ ¼ cup diced avocado

❑ 1 tablespoon salsa

Here's what you do:

1 First heat up the frying pan over low-medium heat and melt butter in it or spray it down with cooking spray.

2 Now crack your egg in a mixing bowl and fork it around until well beaten.

3 Grate your cheese and fork that around in your egg bowl.

4 When your pan is warm, toss in the egg and scramble it. I like to turn the heat on high at this point and then use my stirring spoon to keep stirring the egg around until all parts are cooked. When done, remove and set aside for a moment.

5 Now toss the tortilla onto the frying pan. You can turn the heat off at this point. You just want to warm the tortilla for a moment. Set that aside when done.

6 Now you'll add your toppings. My family's favorites are in the ingredient list. But yours can obviously use anything you'd like. Peanut butter? Weird, but OK, fine. You're in control. Do whatever you like. I'll stick with dicing the tomato and slicing the avocado and adding the egg and toppings to my tortilla. Mmmm. Perfect.

SUPER ACTIVE ATHLETE'S OATMEAL

DIFFICULTY: Easy • **MAKES:** 1 bowl

Emme plays soccer and rides horses and runs those mile-long obstacle courses that make you crawl through mud pits. She is, in a word, active. So of course she needs lots and lots of fuel to keep her going, just like any super active kid—hence, Super Active Athlete's Oatmeal. It's a fast, easy breakfast staple that your child can whip up on her own the morning before a big game or a big day at school. It's loaded with oats and fruit and just the right amount of spice to make everything smell so good. You can find all kinds of instant oatmeals at the store nowadays with a variety of nutritional boosts in them—quinoa, chia, flax, you name it. Try to avoid the ones with flavoring, as they typically contain a boatload of added sugars.

Here's what you need:

TOOLS

❏ Microwave, big microwaveable bowl, measuring cups and spoons, knife, cutting board

INGREDIENTS

❏ 1 packet plain instant oatmeal or one with extra *good* stuff in it, or ¼ cup from your favorite large container

❏ ⅔ cup milk (follow package instructions)

❏ 1 tablespoon chia seeds

❏ 1 apple

❏ 1 pinch brown sugar

❏ 1 pinch cinnamon

❏ 1 tablespoon sliced almonds

Here's what you do:

1. Look, I cheat on this one. I use instant oatmeal packets because they're fast and even the youngest of kids can plop a bowl into a microwave to cook. So open a packet and toss it into a big microwaveable bowl.

2. Now add the milk. Usually it's about ⅔ cup, but follow whatever your own packet of instant oatmeal says.

3. Now sprinkle in the chia seeds and swish them around. Cook oatmeal for about 1 and a half minutes. Again, this is all stuff your sous chef can do.

4. Now chop up the apple into small diced bits. You can sub in blueberries instead or raspberries if that's what your sous chef wants. Let her make the call. We like apples, so here we are.

5. When the oatmeal is done, sprinkle on your sugar and cinnamon. Add apples and almonds. Then mix it around. Your breakfast should smell delicious by now and taste even better. Plus, your little super active athlete has enough fuel to get her through . . . midmorning.

MINI MUFFIN-PAN FRITTATAS

DIFFICULTY: Medium • **MAKES:** 12 frittatas

These adorable single-serving frittatas are like breakfast pies with tomatoes, ham, and cheese. Even better: you're getting some veggies into their breakfast.

Here's what you need:

TOOLS

❏ Oven, oven mitts, 12-muffin pan, mixing bowl, whisk, knife, cutting board, rubber spatula

INGREDIENTS

❏ 6 eggs

❏ ¾ cup milk

❏ 3–4 ounces sliced ham

❏ 6 small mushrooms

❏ ¼ cup grated Parmesan cheese

❏ Salt and pepper pinches

❏ Cooking spray

❏ 12 cherry tomatoes

Here's what you do:

1 Preheat the oven to 350°F.

2 My favorite thing about this is that it creates a wonderful, healthy breakfast or brunch food from just a whole bunch of whisking and dumping. Sit back and read off the recipe while your sous chef does the work. First, crack the eggs into a bowl and whisk them around. Add milk. Whisk again.

3 Now, chop ham and mushrooms into little cubes. Grate your cheese. Add all of that to mix and stir around. Season with salt and pepper and stir again. Easy, right?

4 Spray muffin pan with cooking spray, then fill each muffin cup about ¾ full.

5 Add a whole tomato into the middle of each. Why? Because cooking makes them molten and sweet and delicious; plus kids have a blast dunking them in each muffin cup. Yay!

6 Now cook for about 10–12 minutes. If they're set in the middle, they're done. If they still look runny, cook a few extra minutes until set. Nudge out with rubber spatula and enjoy.

EGGSHELL SCRAMBLES

DIFFICULTY: Easy-medium • **MAKES:** 1 egg

Want to impress the kiddos with a little microwave magic while serving a healthful, tasty breakfast at the same time? This one borders on easy because all you have to do is chip away at the top of an egg, scramble up the insides, and then toss the scramble back into the eggshell. It borders on medium difficulty because chipping away at the top like that without crushing the whole shell can be tricky. I guarantee some amazement while watching this one cook before your eyes.

Here's what you need:

TOOLS

❑ Microwave, knife, mixing bowl, fork, cooking bowl with high sides, paper towels

INGREDIENTS

❑ 1 egg ❑ Coarse salt

Here's what you do:

1 The trick is in chipping away at the egg top—the slightly skinnier end—with a knife and making a few cracks around the whole thing. Use your fingers to sort of pop off the lid. It doesn't have to be removed in one piece and the rest of the eggshell doesn't have to be pristine. Just make sure it's solid enough still to hold some scrambled egg.

2 Dump the inside of the egg into a mixing bowl and fork it around until scrambled.

3 Let's prepare the cooking bowl. Take a paper towel and twist it up and twirl it around until it resembles a snake biting its own tail. See how there's a hole in the middle? Perfect place to rest an egg, wouldn't you say? Place it in the bottom of the bowl.

4 Pour your scramble back into the eggshell. Then put the egg in the paper towel hole. Make sure it's stable and mostly upright.

5 Pop the bowl in the microwave and make sure everyone has a good view. Microwave for 30 seconds. But keep watch starting at 10 seconds. You'll start to see the scramble bubbles bubble even more. At about 15 seconds, you'll see it grow. At 20–25 seconds, the whole thing will sort of rocket out of the shell. Try to stop at the apex of the rocket. No worries if some falls overboard.

6 Remove the egg and sprinkle with coarse salt. Serve with toast sticks if you like and gobble the egg right out of the shell.

THE EASY OMELET

DIFFICULTY: Easy • **MAKES:** 1 omelet

I've seen and had all manner of omelets and, to be honest, I like the big, hearty, French country style just chock-full of ingredients. But you know, sometimes you just want a cheesy, light one that won't weigh you down. This is a nice mix between the fancy and the plain and is a good starter for egg cooking with kids.

Here's what you need:

TOOLS

❑ Stove, medium frying pan, measuring cups and spoons, cheese grater, mixing bowl, fork, rubber spatula

INGREDIENTS

❑ Cheddar cheese, to grate into ¼ cup

❑ ¼ tablespoon butter

❑ 1 egg

Here's what you do:

1 Grate the cheese.

2 Melt the butter over low-medium heat in your pan.

3 Now crack the egg in a mixing bowl and use a fork to break up and stir. Use a tight circular motion with your hand and try to whip in a tiny bit of air. You should see bubbles but not too many.

4 Now dump the egg into the frying pan. Let it cook for a minute and then use spatula to break apart holes in the middle. Tilt pan with one hand until egg mix coats those holes and begins to cook. Cool, huh? Repeat until egg is just barely runny on top.

5 Add grated cheese and roll up one half of the egg onto itself. It should look like almost half of a pie. Now, repeat on the other side. Slide pan around until egg bundle moves. Now, flip and cook for another 30 seconds or so. Plate and enjoy a rich, pretty, creamy omelet.

EGGS-OVER-EASY PEPPERS

DIFFICULTY: Medium-hard • **MAKES:** 1 egg

So now we're going to put all your egg-cooking skills to the test. Remember how you fried the perfect egg by using a splash of water and a lid to steam it? We'll put that on repeat here but turn the recipe up to 11 by adding a ring of red or green bell pepper around the whole shebang. It's a fun twist on fried eggs and adds a touch of vegetable to the mix—always a good thing.

Here's what you need:

TOOLS

❑ Stove, medium frying pan, pot lid, knife, cutting board, spatula, measuring spoon

INGREDIENTS

❑ 1 bell pepper

❑ ¼ tablespoon butter

❑ 1 egg

❑ ½ tablespoon water

Here's what you do:

1 Take a big bell pepper and lay it down so the top is on your right and the bottom is on your left. Slice fully through it. You should have nice big circles at this point. Aim for about ¾" in ring thickness. (Save or use other rings for more eggs—this recipe uses just one.)

2 Now melt butter in pan over low-medium heat.

3 Add pepper ring to middle of frying pan.

4 Crack egg into pepper ring. Try to keep the yolk whole. (Crack into a bowl first to ensure wholeness if your sous chef isn't quite ready to go all in over the pan.)

5 Don't worry if you see egg white ooze out from under pepper. This will probably happen. To prevent it, press down firmly on pepper with spatula until egg is set. Takes a minute or so. If you want it to be perfect, you can also cut off the excess egg ooze later before plating—a trick you don't see on all those Internet photos.

6 Now, add the ½ tablespoon of water to pan and cover pan with lid. Cook for about 1 minute and then check. If the egg is too watery for you, cook a tiny bit longer.

7 Remove with spatula and serve with buttered toast sticks. Yumm. O.

DUTCH BABY

DIFFICULTY: Medium • **MAKES:** 1 big baby

The first time I had a Dutch Baby we were in northern Michigan in a restaurant called the Pancake House. It was a magical experience. The lake was storming and rolling outside and there we were inside the cozy restaurant, tearing into a thin, buttery pancake that had the best consistency I had ever experienced—like something between a crepe and a pancake. I knew right away we had to figure out how to make Dutch Babies at home, and since then it has become a weekend morning staple that never fails to remind me of comfort and family.

Here's what you need:

TOOLS

❏ Stove, oven, large frying pan, oven mitts, measuring cups and spoons, mixing bowls, whisk

INGREDIENTS

❏ ½ cup milk

❏ ½ cup all-purpose flour

❏ 2 eggs

❏ 3 tablespoons sugar

❏ 3 tablespoons butter

❏ Powdered sugar

❏ A couple of lemon wedges

Here's what you do:

1 Preheat the oven to 425°F. This is a hot one.

2 Whisk together the milk, flour, eggs, and sugar. Let your sous chef take the lead. It's as easy as dumping, cracking, and whisking. Stir until smooth.

3 Melt all your butter in your large frying pan over medium heat, tilting the pan until the butter is everywhere.

4 Now pour in your batter. Just let it cook for a minute without touching it. No stirring or flipping here.

5 After a minute, grab your oven mitts and throw the whole frying pan into the oven. Cook for 12–14 minutes or until it's golden and puffed up like a pancake you've never seen before. It grows quite nicely and then shrinks quickly once you remove it. Let cool a minute and then slice with a knife and put enormous wedges on your eating plates. Sprinkle with a dash of sugar and a squeeze of lemon. Ahh, that's the stuff.

CUP O' PANCAKE

DIFFICULTY: Easy • **MAKES:** 1 pancake in a cup

As the main maker of kitchen messes and the main cleaner of said messes, I've come to appreciate quick and easy meals that don't require a ton of prep or cleaning. Enter: The pancake in a cup. You toss all your ingredients in a mug, stir it around, and zap it in the microwave. Throw in a pat of butter and drizzle on a little syrup and you have a fun breakfast treat that doesn't require much cleanup. That's my kind of breakfast.

Here's what you need:

TOOLS

❑ Microwave, large mug, fork, measuring spoons

INGREDIENTS

❑ 4 tablespoons all-purpose flour

❑ ¼ teaspoon baking powder

❑ 2 tablespoons milk

❑ 1 egg

❑ 1 teaspoon sugar

❑ ½ tablespoon butter

❑ Syrup

Here's what you do:

1 It's really as easy as tossing the first five ingredients into the mug and stirring around with a fork until it's nice and smooth. It should go without saying that your kid can do it all.

2 Now, throw it in the microwave for 50 seconds. I've found that 1 minute is just too much and 45 seconds is undercooked. But microwave power varies so give it a try at 50 first and see what happens. It should sort of rise out of the mug by 3"–4", but they generally don't fall over or go much higher. They do, however, shrink pretty quickly when you pull them out. Have your sous chef watch, because it's amazing to see a little pancake turn into a cup rocket. Fun times.

3 When you pull the mug out, quickly add a pat of butter and let it fall to the sides where it will melt faster. Now drizzle on some syrup and serve the cup as is. You can take the cake out and slice it up, but it's more fun to eat out of the cup.

GOURDGEOUS PUMPKIN WAFFLES

DIFFICULTY: Medium • **MAKES:** 8–10 waffles

I tend to eat pretty healthily during most of the year, and because I'm in charge of most of the meals, my family does as well. But when fall hits, all bets are off. So pumpkin waffles have become a family hit. They've got a delicious outside crunch and a sweet, pumpkin-flavored creaminess on the inside. Add in some whipped cream and a little syrup and you've got just the thing for a cold fall or winter weekend morning.

Here's what you need:

TOOLS

- ❏ Waffle iron, measuring cups and spoons, large mixing bowl, medium mixing bowl, stirring spoon, whisk

INGREDIENTS

- ❏ Cooking spray
- ❏ 1½ cups flour
- ❏ 1 tablespoon baking powder
- ❏ Pinch salt
- ❏ 1 teaspoon cinnamon
- ❏ ¼ teaspoon nutmeg
- ❏ 3 eggs
- ❏ 1¾ cups milk
- ❏ ½ cup canned pumpkin purée (not pie filling)
- ❏ ¼ cup vegetable oil
- ❏ 2 tablespoons maple syrup

Here's what you do:

1. Spray your waffle iron with cooking spray and then heat it up.

2. In a large mixing bowl, combine flour, baking powder, salt, and spices.

3. In a different bowl, whisk together your eggs, milk, pumpkin purée, oil, and syrup until well mixed.

4. Now pour your liquids over your dry and whisk together until you have a nice smooth batter. Pause for a moment and smell that heavenly aroma of pumpkin and spice. I never get . . . *gourd* of that smell.

5. Pour the batter in your waffle iron and wait for your birdy whistle or light to go on.

PIGS IN THE PEN

DIFFICULTY: Easy • **MAKES:** 2 dozen piggies

You probably remember this one well; it's a childhood classic. The thing is, it's ridiculously easy—as in, easy enough for kids to create their own childhood classics. I like to mix these up by using maple syrup breakfast sausage instead of sliced hot dogs or mini Vienna sausages, because I think they taste better this way. But really, use whatever type of rolled sausage meat you like. Slap on some pre-made biscuit dough, and you're in for a fun morning, promise. (You can save a few for lunchboxes, too.)

Here's what you need:

TOOLS

❏ Oven, oven mitts, cookie sheet, knife, cutting board

INGREDIENTS

❏ 1 roll of refrigerated biscuit dough

❏ 8 maple syrup sausages

❏ Cheddar cheese and maple syrup (optional)

Here's what you do:

1 Preheat the oven to 350°F.

2 Unroll the biscuit dough. You may need to help your sous chef with this unless he's old enough. I always get spooked by the pop and the razor-thin edges of the unrolled can. Careful, yo.

3 Cut the sausages in roughly 3"-long segments.

4 Cut the dough to form strips. Roll each strip around a piggy and place on the cookie sheet. Make sure the flap is on the bottom when you put the piggies on the cookie sheet, as the cooking will seal it all shut without having to use toothpicks.

5 Now cook for 10–15 minutes or until golden, crispy brown.

DAD TIP

If you want, add a tiny strip of cheese alongside the sausage before you roll everything up. It makes for a gooey, sausage-cheese fest. Dip the piggies into syrup and you're golden, Ponyboy.

SWEET CANDY BACON FLAPJACKS

DIFFICULTY: Medium • **MAKES:** 12 flapjacks

Any time I go to a diner that serves bacon pancakes, I order them. Some are done almost perfectly. The bacon is a complement and almost an afterthought, and there's that delightful mix of salty and sweet, smoky and syrupy. You still get your light and fluffy pancakes, but they have a just-right smoky crunch to them. Of course, there's the flip side as well. I've had bacon cakes that tasted as if the diner cooked up a thud of dough around a heaping mound of Bac-Os Bits. Not good. In this recipe, I'm going for the former, and giving you the perfect recipe to use up any of your leftover Sweet Candy Bacon.

Here's what you need:

TOOLS

❑ Stove, large frying pan or griddle pan, measuring cups and spoons, mixing bowls, whisk, spatula

INGREDIENTS

❑ 1 cup all-purpose flour

❑ 1 tablespoon sugar

❑ 1½ teaspoons baking powder

❑ ½ teaspoon baking soda

❑ Pinch salt

❑ 1 egg

❑ 1¼ cups buttermilk

❑ 3 tablespoons maple syrup

❑ 1 tablespoon butter, melted

❑ 1 tablespoon butter, not melted

❑ 2 strips cooked bacon

❑ Extra syrup for dipping or pouring

Here's what you do:

1 In a large bowl, combine the flour, sugar, baking powder, baking soda, and a pinch of salt.

2 Lightly whisk egg in a separate bowl. Then add egg, buttermilk, syrup, and melted butter to your flour mix. Whisk until blended and smooth.

3 Now heat your pan on low heat and butter it all over.

4 Pour pancake mix into pan—usually 4 fit on a griddle at a time.

5 Break up your finished, crispy bacon into little bits—about the size of M&M's—and dot them on the top of the cooking flapjack. Use as many as you'd like, but I tend to go for 6–8 per flapjack to avoid over-chewiness. You want a hint of bacon here, not a whole pig. (But use as much as you like, it's your pancake.)

6 When the sides of the flapjacks are cooked and golden, flip and cook for another minute or two.

7 Unless you're serving them straight from the pan, plop them onto a plate and then toss them into an oven set at 200°F or lower. It keeps everything toasty until you're ready to serve. If you can wait that long . . .

LUNCH

3

When I was a kid, lunch involved a mad rush into the nearest house of any friend I happened to be playing with at the time. A quick sandwich. A gulp of milk. Maybe an apple. And then *poof*, we disappeared again—off to explore the neighborhood some more. Now, as a parent, I know well the messy aftermath a horde of hungry children can leave behind. But man, is it ever worth it.

In these recipes, you'll find lunches for a busy day, for a lazy weekend, and for DIY school lunches that will put a smile on any kid's face. Lunch can sometimes be overlooked as a quick grab-and-go meal—and to be sure, there are some ideas for fast, fun foods in here—but I tried to provide some family favorites that involve a little more attention. So whether you're facing that hungry horde or just chilling on a quiet day, hopefully you'll find something yummy to make together.

GRILLED CHEESE ROLLS

DIFFICULTY: Easy-medium • **MAKES:** 1 roll

This is a fun twist on the lunchtime classic that allows you to bend and twist traditional ingredients into something new and special. It's a great way to teach your little chef that even the most classic of ingredients can be experimented with to create new ways of presenting meals.

Here's what you need:

TOOLS

❑ Stove, frying pan, knife, cutting board, rolling pin, spatula or tongs

INGREDIENTS

❑ 1 slice white or whole wheat bread

❑ 1 slice American cheese

❑ 1 tablespoon butter

Here's what you do:

1 Heat your pan to medium and get it warm while you slice the crusts off your bread.

2 Next, take your rolling pin and gently roll the bread until it's flat and malleable. Make sure it's flat enough to roll but not squished so much that it breaks apart when you lift it. Think gentle steamroller.

3 Now add your slice of cheese on top of the bread and roll. Make it as tight as you can. When it's rolled up (but feels like it might actually unroll), put the rolled part down on the cutting board and press down with your hand, or use your fingers to pinch the bread together. Cooking should quickly solve any mistakes.

4 Melt the butter in your pan and add sandwich so that the seam is face down in the butter. The grilling should seal everything just fine.

5 Use your spatula or tongs to turn roll in the butter until it's golden brown all over—about a minute or so for each move.

6 When cheese begins to melt out of the ends, you're good to go. Remove, slice if you'd like (or don't), and serve with tomato soup for a toasty lunch on a cold day.

TUNA FISH SHAPES

DIFFICULTY: Easy • **MAKES:** 1 sandwich

Something magical happens when you break out the cookie cutters. Eyes go wide and anticipatory smiles are already at work. This recipe is simple enough for just about any kid to do on his own and puts a special, personal touch on an otherwise ordinary lunch staple.

Here's what you need:

TOOLS

❑ Bowl, fork, measuring spoons, cookie cutter shapes of choice, cutting board

INGREDIENTS

❑ ½ can tuna fish

❑ 1 tablespoon pickle relish

❑ 1 tablespoon mayo

❑ 2 slices bread of choice

Here's what you do:

1 Make a tuna fish sandwich like you ordinarily would. Add ½ can tuna, relish, and mayo to bowl and stir. I save the leftover tuna for myself to eat out of the can as a pre- or post-workout snack, or you can use in the Tuna Orange Dip. Yum.

2 Slather a thin layer on bread and top with other slice of bread.

3 Let your kitchen helper take the lead on cutting the sandwich, including picking a cookie cutter and pressing out a perfect shape. Just plop out onto plate and don't forget the inverse shape image left behind. That's fun to eat as well.

CLASSIC QUESADILLA

DIFFICULTY: Easy • **MAKES:** 1 quesadilla

Want a go-to classic you can make in about 5 minutes? Try a cheesy quesadilla! It's a lot like a grilled cheese sandwich—you're melting cheese between layers of flour product—but the mouth-feel is slightly chewier and denser and the way the cheese melts into your mouth is something to inspire drooling daydreams. Although this recipe doesn't call for it, you can easily doctor it up with slices of chicken or vegetables in addition to cheese. Serve with salsa and sour cream or avocado and suddenly you have an amazing lunch.

Here's what you need:

TOOLS
❏ Stove, frying pan, cheese grater, spatula

INGREDIENTS
❏ Cheddar or queso fresco cheese, to grate into ¼ cup

❏ ½ tablespoon butter

❏ 2 flour or corn tortillas

Here's what you do:

1 Warm your pan to medium heat while you grate ¼ cup of cheese, an amount about the size of your sous chef's fist.

2 Melt the butter in your pan and add 1 tortilla. Top with all your cheese, spreading it out evenly, and then add second tortilla on top.

3 Cook each side for about 2 to 3 minutes, or until nice and golden brown. You should be able to lift the tortilla with your fingers or spatula to test for melty cheese. When it's ready, use the spatula to remove. Let stand for about 30 seconds before cutting across the quesadilla up and down and side to side so that you have 4 big triangles. You can cut more if you like or not at all. Up to you.

MINI BURRITOS

DIFFICULTY: Medium • **MAKES:** 8 mini burritos

I love visiting our neighborhood taqueria a few blocks away. As soon as you walk in the door, you're hit with wondrous smells of meat, beans, cheese, and a sweet overtone of icy cold aguas fresca. What's even better is the customization available; you can have a burrito or taco any way you like. This recipe seeks to replicate that experience by putting the kids in charge of their lunch. There are a lot of ingredients here, but you can use less or more, depending on what your chef wants.

Here's what you need:

TOOLS

❏ Stove, microwave, large frying pan, small frying pan, measuring cups and spoons, spatula or spoon, knife, cutting board, lots of small bowls, lots of spoons, cheese grater, can opener

INGREDIENTS

❏ 1 pound ground beef

❏ 2 tablespoons water

❏ 1 tablespoon taco seasoning (if you don't have any, just use salt and pepper—and maybe a pinch of chili powder if you have it)

❏ 1 tomato

❏ 1 white onion

❏ Cheddar or queso fresco cheese, to grate into ½ cup

❏ 1 can black beans

❏ ½ cup salsa

❏ ¼ cup shredded lettuce

❏ 1 splash oil

❏ 8 corn or flour tortillas, the smallest you can find

❏ 1 avocado

❏ Cilantro, to taste

Here's what you do:

1 First, brown the ground beef in the large frying pan. Drain excess fat as it nears completion and then add water and taco seasoning, or whatever you'd like to season it. Salt and pepper alone will do the trick.

2 While the beef is cooking, create an assembly line of ingredients. Dice tomato and put into a small bowl. Finely chop onion and put into a bowl. Let the kids deal with watery eyes but get ready to jump in. (Try swim goggles if any of you is tearing up too much.) Grate cheese. Bowl. Heat black beans in microwave (1–2 minutes). Bowl. Salsa. Bowl. You get the idea. Have your sous chef prepare all the ingredients she wants to eat and put in small bowls for easier assembly in the next steps.

3 When your beef is done and in a bowl of its own, heat up a small frying pan and add a very small splash of oil. Put tortilla down to warm up. You're just warming it up here and making it easier to fold and slightly tastier, not cooking it or making it crisp.

4 When your tortilla is warm, remove and put on plate. Add beef, tomatoes, onion, cheese, avocado if you like, cilantro—you name it. There's no wrong way to make these. But it's a lot easier to assemble if you have your ingredients ready to go, and the kids seem to like the control aspect of it all. Plus, it's fun. Repeat with as many tortillas as you have.

DAD TIP

You can, of course, use any meat you'd like or have on hand. Thinly sliced steak (use leftovers if you have any) is delicious. Pork carnitas is always a winner too. Whatever you choose, this is a great recipe for teaching how to clean up since you'll use a lot of bowls. Show your chef how to rinse dishes and stack them properly in the dishwasher.

TUNA ORANGE DIP

DIFFICULTY: Easy-medium • **MAKES:** 1 cup

I know what you're thinking: tuna orange . . . *dip*? Yeah, it sounds worse than it is. Trust me. This is a super easy lunch or snack that you can make in a flash and doesn't require many tools or ingredients. Plus, it smells absolutely wonderful—like the sea and sweet citrus. It's a winner for sure, despite the name. (Maybe you guys can come up with a better one? Go for it.)

Here's what you need:

TOOLS
❏ Small serving bowl, microplane zester, knife, measuring spoons, fork

INGREDIENTS
❏ 1 can tuna fish

❏ 1 orange, washed

❏ 1 tablespoon olive oil

❏ Salt and pepper to taste

❏ Big handful of crackers of choice

Here's what you do:

1 Dump the can of tuna fish into a small serving bowl (or use leftover tuna from the Tuna Fish Shapes recipe in this chapter).

2 Grab your orange and your microplane zester and carefully zest the top layer of orange onto the tuna. Slice open orange and squeeze a tiny bit of juice into bowl.

3 Add oil and salt and pepper to taste and stir around. Zest a teeny bit more orange onto dip to finish, along with a few more shakes of pepper.

4 Use crackers of choice to dip and give it a try. Good, right? Told ya.

SARDINES AND TOAST

DIFFICULTY: Easy • **MAKES:** 3–4 toasts

Apparently I've passed on my taste for salty brined fish to my daughter, who came up with this easy recipe and loves it. Just like some people like anchovies on their pizza and some people think that's just crazy talk, sardines are an acquired taste. But you never know if your kid likes them unless you try. They're chock-full of wonderful fats and tons of protein, so give them a go and see what your little chef thinks. We're big fans. You may be too.

Here's what you need:

TOOLS
❑ Toaster, fork

INGREDIENTS
❑ 1 can sardines of choice

❑ 3–4 slices bread of choice

Here's what you do:

1 This is a great recipe for teaching kids how to use a toaster or toaster oven. Pop in your slices and open the sardine can while the bread is doing its business.

2 When the bread is ready, put it on a plate and fork out a sardine and serve on top of your toast. Emme likes sardines cured in maple syrup. But we've found that all kinds work well.

PB&J BITES

DIFFICULTY: Ridiculously easy • **MAKES:** 1 sandwich worth of bites

Peanut butter and jelly sandwiches were a summertime staple for me as a kid. It was our version of fast food, and made with the proper ingredients, a PB&J can be quite good for you. (Check your jars: Peanut butter doesn't need sugar or palm oil. Try the health food section at the store for a healthier option, or grind your own if the store has a grinding machine on hand. *So* good.) Had I learned this simple trick earlier, my summertime lunches would have been even cooler. Seriously, it's as simple as slicing and dicing. It does wonders for making quick lunches go down even faster. Then you can get back to playing.

Here's what you need:

TOOLS
- ❏ Knife, cutting board

INGREDIENTS
- ❏ 2 slices bread
- ❏ 1 tablespoon peanut butter
- ❏ 1 tablespoon jelly or jam of choice

Here's what you do:

1. Look, you and I know how to make a PB&J. I get that. It's easy. So let the kids do this from start to finish. Even the youngest child can do this. Simply spread peanut butter and jelly on bread and top with the other slice of bread. Done. Awesome. Now let's cut.

2. Take your knife and cut as many tiny bites as you like or as your sous chef wants. Again, you can do this easily; let the kids try. Think of all the times in the near future when you'll be able to say, "Hungry? OK, go fix yourself some PB&J bites."

DAD TIP

Next time you're shopping, look around for the peanut butter grinding machine. The kids love to do this and it's fun to watch the grinding in action. Plus, you can have a cool little talk about what you *really* need to make peanut butter. Grab a jar of regular peanut butter and compare the ingredients to what you find in the grinding machine. I think the kids will be surprised.

SLOPPYISH JOES

DIFFICULTY: Medium • **MAKES:** 8 Joes

On the surface, it seems like this recipe has a lot of ingredients and can become tedious for little chefs. But in reality, you're just cooking ground beef and dumping in a lot of stuff for flavor. I like that it doesn't require a lot of cleanup. Kids like that it tastes so good and that they made it. Another win-win.

Here's what you need:

TOOLS

- ❏ Stove, large frying pan with lid, spoon or spatula, knife, cutting board, measuring cups and spoons

INGREDIENTS

- ❏ 1 onion
- ❏ 1 tablespoon oil
- ❏ Salt and pepper to taste
- ❏ 1 pound ground beef
- ❏ 2 cups frozen hash browns
- ❏ 1 cup ketchup
- ❏ 1 tablespoon Worcestershire sauce, or steak sauce of choice
- ❏ 1 tablespoon tomato paste
- ❏ 8 hamburger buns

Here's what you do:

1. Start with the onion. Dice it into very small cubes and cook in the frying pan with oil over low heat for 15 minutes or until soft. Salt and pepper them occasionally.

2. Now add ground beef and brown on medium heat.

3. Now add hash browns and cook for about 5 minutes.

4. Here's the fun part: the ingredient dump. Add ketchup, Worcestershire sauce, and tomato paste. Cover the frying pan and simmer on low heat for about 20–25 minutes.

5. When done, stir around and spoon onto hamburger buns and enjoy with a side of Rainbow Salad (see recipe in Chapter 5) or any delicious veggies of choice.

 DAD TIP

You can make this even easier by substituting a ready-made Sloppy Joe canned mix, but check the sugar and sodium content on those first. They can be off the charts.

MONTE CRISTO

DIFFICULTY: Medium • **MAKES:** 1 sandwich

There's something irresistible about a good Monte Cristo. They're sweet and salty, loaded with ham and cheese and eggy French toast and then topped with sugar and dipped into jam. My all-time favorite Monte Cristo came from the Blue Bayou restaurant in Disneyland. The coolness of eating in a restaurant right inside the Pirates of the Caribbean was somehow eclipsed by a sandwich that tasted like a miracle on a plate. This one is a modified version that doesn't require a deep fryer, or a popular theme park. Thankfully, it tastes just as good.

Here's what you need:

TOOLS
❑ Stove, baking dish or pie plate, whisk, measuring cups and spoons, large frying pan, spatula

INGREDIENTS
❑ 2 eggs

❑ ¼ cup milk

❑ 1 teaspoon cinnamon

❑ 2 slices bread

❑ 1 tablespoon butter, divided

❑ 1 slice ham

❑ 1 slice Swiss cheese

❑ 1 pinch powdered sugar

❑ 2 tablespoons raspberry jam

Here's what you do:

1 The first and most difficult thing is making the French toast batter. The rest is downhill. In the baking dish or any pie plate or bowl suitable for dunking bread in an egg bath, whisk together eggs, milk, and cinnamon.

2 Now heat up the frying pan to medium and soak your bread in the milky egg mixture while the frying pan heats.

3 Melt ½ tablespoon butter in frying pan and put the 2 bread slices side by side. Cook for about 3 minutes or until golden brown.

4 Lift both slices and put remaining butter in frying pan before turning bread over and laying it down again.

5 Once the other side of the bread is cooking, put ham and cheese slices on 1 piece of bread. Let them begin to warm.

6 After another 3 minutes, lift the empty bread slice onto the ham and cheese. Flip whole sandwich and cook for about a minute, then flip it again and cook for another minute or so, making sure the cheese gets melty.

7 Plate sandwich, cut into triangles, and sprinkle with powdered sugar. Serve with a side of raspberry jam and get ready to enjoy a lunch treat that will surely become a fond foodie memory.

CHEESE-CRUSTED FISH FILLETS

DIFFICULTY: Hard • **MAKES:** 4 servings

The cool thing about this recipe is that you can use either fresh or frozen fish fillets. I'd go with fresh if you can get it, but if not, frozen still works great. Either way, try to use a nice firm white fish—a turbot or roughy. But don't be afraid to use what you have or what's fresh. In the end, you're going to have a wonderful texture contrast between firm, sweet white fish and gooey, cheesy goodness. This is always a hit.

Here's what you need:

TOOLS

❏ Oven, baking pan, oven mitts, large mixing bowl, knife, cutting board, measuring spoons, stirring spoon

INGREDIENTS

❏ Cooking spray or ½ tablespoon butter

❏ 1 pound white fish fillets

❏ 1 (4-ounce) package softened cream cheese

❏ 1 garlic clove, smashed and minced

❏ 2 green onions, sliced

❏ 1 teaspoon lemon juice

❏ 1 tablespoon chopped parsley for garnish

Here's what you do:

1 Preheat the oven to 350°F and then spray baking pan with cooking spray.

2 Spread the fillets in the pan in a single layer.

3 In a large mixing bowl, combine the cream cheese, minced garlic, sliced green onions, and lemon juice. Mix well.

4 Now spread the cheese mixture over the fillets, coating them as well as possible. Don't be afraid to get messy.

5 Bake for 35 or so minutes, or until fish is lightly browned on top and fully cooked. The cheese should be melty and brown and crunchy in places. Serve with parsley as a garnish sprinkled on top.

DAD TIP

I always thought garlic was a pain to cut— and then I learned to smash it to smither- eens. Remove cloves from garlic head easily by placing the whole head on a cutting board and smushing it with your palm. Go on, get all *Road House* on it. Pain don't hurt. Once you have a clove free, don't even worry about peeling it. Just place on cutting board and rest flat side of knife on top of it. Press down on knife until the clove is smushed. Remove skin and then mince away. Don't forget to use only one cutting board for gar- lic, as it can stink up other foods. Just select a small cutting board and put it aside, using it only for garlic and onion chopping.

SLAMMIN' SANDWICH SKEWERS

DIFFICULTY: Easy • **MAKES:** 2 skewers

This recipe goes hand in hand with the PB&J Bites (see recipe in this chapter). It's just a new take on an old staple and adheres to my philosophy when it comes to kids and food: Put anything on a skewer and they'll at least try it.

Here's what you need:

TOOLS

❏ Knife, cutting board, bamboo skewers

INGREDIENTS

❏ 2 slices bread

❏ 1 tablespoon peanut butter

❏ 1 teaspoon jam or jelly

Here's what you do:

1 Have your kids make a PB&J sandwich. Tell them to go light on jelly to avoid goopy skewers.

2 Cut into bite-sized cubes.

3 Place bites onto skewers—about 3 or 4 cubes per skewer. Serve with a side of milk and some apples and you have a lunch made in fun heaven.

BAGEL PIZZA BITES

DIFFICULTY: Medium • **MAKES:** 4 mini pizzas

Walk by a freezer section with a kid and it's like they've visited food Disneyland. They think, "Oh my God, chicken shaped like *dinosaurs*!" Or "pizza . . . *tubes*?! Wow!" And you think, "Now *that* can't be good for you." Indeed. I like mini bagel pizzas because you can control the ingredients and not have to worry about added junk while making something yummy and fun together.

Here's what you need:

TOOLS

- ❏ Oven, cookie sheet, oven mitts, knife, cutting board, cheese grater, can opener, spoon

INGREDIENTS

- ❏ 2 whole wheat bagels
- ❏ 1 jar pizza sauce
- ❏ ½ cup grated mozzarella cheese
- ❏ 2 mushrooms, sliced

Here's what you do:

1. Preheat the oven to 400°F.

2. Slice the bagels in half. Once you have 4 slices, cut each in half again to have 8. You can also use bagel thins or sandwich thins as makeshift pizza crusts. They're typically available in the bread section. These will be your pizza crusts.

3. Let your pizza chef choose what to put on each crust circle. Just slather on a spoonful or two of pizza sauce, then sprinkle on cheese and top with any ingredients you like. Emme likes mushrooms on her pizza, so that's what I listed in the ingredients as a suggestion.

4. Cook for about 5–7 minutes or until cheese is nice and melty and the ingredients start to bubble. You can cook for just shy of 5 minutes to ensure a softer crust.

CHEESY CHICKEN FINGERS

DIFFICULTY: Hardish • **MAKES:** 4 servings

This is sort of a boneless version of your favorite drumsticks—only using white meat and copious amounts of delicious Parmesan cheese. Chicken fingers are the ubiquitous child's menu mealtime favorite, and I like to show this recipe to kids so they know how to make it even tastier all on their own.

Here's what you need:

TOOLS

❑ Stove, large frying pan, knife, cutting board, 2 pie pans, measuring cups and spoons, whisk, cheese grater, 2 sets of tongs, wax paper

INGREDIENTS

❑ 2 boneless, skinless chicken breasts

❑ 1 egg, beaten

❑ 3 tablespoons olive oil, divided

❑ ¼ cup milk

❑ 1 tablespoon water

❑ 2 tablespoons flour

❑ ½ cup breadcrumbs

❑ ½ teaspoon salt

❑ ¼ teaspoon pepper

❑ ¼ cup Parmesan cheese, grated

Here's what you do:

1 First, cut the chicken into strips. You know what a chicken finger looks like. Do that. Make them as uniform as possible so they cook evenly.

2 In one pie pan, whisk together egg, 1 tablespoon of the oil, milk, and water. This is your chicken bath. Soak all the fingers in it.

3 In the other pie pan, combine flour, breadcrumbs, salt, pepper, and cheese. Mix.

4 Use one set of tongs to lift chicken from bath and drop gently into flour mix. Use the other set to roll chicken around in the mix and then remove and place on sheet of wax paper. Repeat process until all your chicken fingers are dunked and dipped.

5 Now, for the frying. Hot oil bubbles and pops and splatters, so kids might not be up to the task. In a large frying pan, heat remaining 2 tablespoons oil over medium-high heat. Cook chicken in hot oil, turning and flipping until done—10 or so minutes.

DAD TIP

Should your oil catch on fire, NEVER use water to douse the flames. Instead, dump baking soda on it.

ORANGE YOU GLAD YOU LIKE CHICKEN?

DIFFICULTY: Medium • **MAKES:** 4 servings

This delightfully tasty dish with hints of orange and mustard takes me back to childhood and watching all the pros on PBS whipping up decadent dishes. This was an era before cooking show hosts screamed at you and made you feel on edge. I always used to watch these fun shows and then head to the kitchen to experiment afterward. Here's a classic from all that experimentation. Kids like the familiar flavor of orange as a variation on boring baked chicken.

Here's what you need:

TOOLS

❑ Oven, large baking dish or oven-safe frying pan with high rim, oven mitts, measuring cups and spoons, knife, cutting board

INGREDIENTS

❑ 4 skinless, boneless chicken breasts

❑ 2 tablespoons Dijon mustard

❑ ¾ cup orange juice

❑ 1 tablespoon butter

❑ 3 tablespoons brown sugar

Here's what you do:

1. Preheat the oven to 350°F.

2. This one just requires dumping lots of stuff into a baking pan. Practically any kid can do this. First, put chicken in pan.

3. Spoon mustard over each breast and slather it around to coat.

4. Pour orange juice gently over chicken. You don't want to wash the mustard off but just sort of give the chicken a nice little shower. The juice then fills the pan.

5. Cut the butter into little cubes. Then top the chicken with all those cubes.

6. Sprinkle each breast with brown sugar. Don't worry if it's not the evenest layer you've ever seen. Let the kids do all this. It's fun and they made it.

7. Now, cook for about 30–35 minutes. I like to serve this with rice, as it soaks up excess juices. Mmmm.

PASTA ALLA CARBONARA

DIFFICULTY: Medium-hard • **MAKES:** 4 servings

This is one of those warm, comforting foods that could easily work for dinner as well as lunch. It's simple to make, only has a few ingredients, and—although this may well be sacrilege to say—sort of reminds me of a mac and cheese on yummy steroids. There are a lot of moving parts here—preparing sauce and bacon while water boils and then spaghetti cooks—but each step is relatively easy and is just right for a burgeoning chef to attempt on her own.

Here's what you need:

TOOLS

❏ Stove, large pot, large frying pan, knife, cutting board, strainer, stirring spoons, mixing bowl, fork or whisk

INGREDIENTS

❏ 8 cups water

❏ Salt

❏ 4 strips bacon

❏ 2 tablespoons olive oil, divided

❏ 1 (1-pound) package spaghetti

❏ 2 eggs

❏ 1 cup freshly grated Parmesan cheese (best you can find)

❏ Pepper, freshly ground

Here's what you do:

1 Heat up salted water in a large pot.

2 As the water heats up, chop your bacon into bite-sized pieces and then heat up the large frying pan on medium heat.

3 Add a small drizzle of your oil to the pan and then add bacon. Check to see if the water is boiling yet.

4 Let bacon get nice and crispy, stirring a few times. Add spaghetti to water and cook for 9–11 minutes, or whatever your package says.

5 So now you have the spaghetti boiling and the bacon crisping. It's time to work on the sauce. You want it to be totally ready to go by the time your spaghetti is done. Timing is key here, as you'll be cooking the egg with the heat of the spaghetti alone. So, in a mixing bowl, combine 2 eggs and the cheese. Whisk or fork it around until smooth.

6 Here's the fun part. When your spaghetti is done, drain it (reserve a few tablespoons of water in the pot—in other words, don't dump it all out).

7 Now quickly add the spaghetti to the bacon pan and stir it around so the fat coats the noodles.

8 Turn off the heat and add your egg and cheese mixture. If you leave the heat on, the egg can scramble. You just want it to cook by the heat of the noodles alone. Stir it around a fair bit.

9 Plate your spaghetti and offer a fresh grind of pepper to anyone who wants it. Get ready for a warm, comforting treat.

SOMEWHERE OVER THE RAINBOW PASTA

DIFFICULTY: Medium • **MAKES:** 4 servings

There are a lot of recipes on the interwebs for rainbow pasta, but few seem to tell you just how time intensive and annoying they are, or that there is a lot of work happening behind the scenes to make it all so colorful and pretty. When I first started this, I was annoyed that the dish always turned into a curmudgeonly muddle of greenish-brown pasta, not the Rainbow Brite lunch we were after. So I'm breaking it all down here with tips and tricks I learned to make rainbow pasta that actually looks colorful and tastes good. When you master it, it's no-brainy. There are just lots of little steps, so I'd save this for a rainy-day craft or special party. It's not a go-to quick-time lunch. But it sure puts a smile on little faces.

Here's what you need:

TOOLS

❑ Stove, large pot, strainer, 4 big plastic bags, serving spoons or forks, 4 serving bowls

INGREDIENTS

❑ 1 package pasta of your choice (I like small bites, like bow-tie pasta)

❑ 8 cups water

❑ Butter and cheese for topping

❑ 4 food colorings of choice—red, blue, yellow, green, let's say

Here's what you do:

1 Oh, it starts out so easy . . . boil your water and cook your pasta. It usually takes about 8–11 minutes, depending on the kind you use.

2 Now, here come the tricks. Strain the pasta and really cool it down. It has to be cold. Just keep the pasta in the strainer and rinse it with water a whole bunch. Let it rest. Rinse it some more. Seriously, I hope you get the point. Room temp with no heat to it all will work best, so just keep it all cold under the water. When you think it's good, shake off excess water.

3 Now, divide the pasta into your 4 bags. Add a healthy dose of food coloring to each bag and mix around with spoons until you're happy with the color. Seal the bags and just let them sit awhile. If you're anxious to eat, go at least 2 minutes. If not, let them brew in the bag for 5 minutes or so. Move the pasta around within the bag every once in a while.

4 Here's a cool tip. Everyone seems to say you can dump all the bags into a big serving bowl, but I find this creates a muddled stew of grossness. Instead, I've learned to just scoop out a tiny portion of green and put it directly into the bowl the kiddo will be eating out of. Then add blue, then red, then yellow. Mix it in the individual serving bowls, not in a big one. Make sense? Good.

5 Once you have your rainbow bowls plated, nuke 'em in the microwave with butter to reheat. Usually 1 minute works fine. Top with grated cheese. This sort of dulls the rainbow effect and you don't need it, but it *is* pasta and you want it to be delicious, not just cool looking. Or do whatever your kiddo wants. There's always that option, too.

CHEESY RICE–STUFFED TOMATOES

DIFFICULTY: Medium • **MAKES:** 6 tomatoes

This dish always reminds me of the inside of a good burrito. There's cheese and rice and a hint of garlic, and they're all combined in a hot, gooey flow of awesome sauce. Only, it's all contained in a perfectly cooked tomato. These tomatoes are excellent for meals or as the perfect complement to your Balsamic Steak Bites (see recipe in Chapter 5).

Here's what you need:

TOOLS

❏ Oven, microwave, cookie sheet, oven mitts, knife, cutting board, mixing bowl, cheese grater, measuring cups and spoons, stirring spoons

INGREDIENTS

❏ 6 medium-sized tomatoes

❏ 1 clove garlic

❏ ½ cup grated mozzarella cheese, divided

❏ 3 tablespoons olive oil

❏ 1 cup cooked rice

Here's what you do:

1 Preheat the oven to 400°F.

2 Slice off the tops of your tomatoes and scoop out the innards. Pretend you're making cups. Because, I suppose, you *are*. Set the tomatoes upside down on a plate to drain them. Plus they sort of plump out, which makes them easier to fill.

3 Now crush the garlic clove and mince it. Add to mixing bowl with most of your cheese (save a bit for topping), oil, and rice. I like to use those little cheaty packets of microwave rice because it's ready in 90 seconds and doesn't require more pots and pans.

4 Now gently stuff your rice and cheese mixture into tomatoes. You want to fill them and pack them gently. It's OK to fill up over the rim. It should go without saying that kids love doing this part.

5 Now sprinkle with more cheese and pop into oven. Cook for 25–30 minutes, or until cheese is nice and brown. You want the garlic inside to be cooked, and the rice and cheese mixture to be nice and gooey.

DIY BENTO BOXES

DIFFICULTY: Easy • **MAKES:** 1 packed lunch you don't even need to worry about

Here's the thing with this one: You have to let go. Just let. it. go. (Sorry for the earworm.) Even your preschooler can put this lunch together. I like to set out a batch of ingredients for a school lunch and then let the kiddo pack it all up. There might be rice, greens, some form of protein, perhaps a sweet. The idea is that I supply the good food options and she packs her own lunch in delightfully compartmentalized containers—the perfect DIY bento box. I've found that the more the kiddos make themselves, the more they actually eat. If you can, find a lunch container system that allows for separate packing. They're pretty easy to find nowadays. But you can always divide everything up into separate plastic bags instead. This is an ideal recipe for using up last night's leftovers. As an example, that's what I'm doing here.

Here's what you need:

TOOLS
- ❏ Knife, cutting board, microwave, lots of little bowls, compartmentalized lunch container or individual plastic bags

INGREDIENTS
- ❏ ¼ cup cooked rice
- ❏ 3–4 ounces protein (leftover salmon here!)
- ❏ 2 ounces frozen edamame
- ❏ 3 baby carrots
- ❏ 3 big strawberries
- ❏ Small handful blueberries

Here's what you do:

1 If your little chef can do it all from start to finish, let her. Otherwise, you do this part: Set out the ingredients in small bowls.

2 Then bring in your sous chef and have her pack everything into its own container. Yes, it really *is* that easy. Yes, I feel guilty for even including this recipe. But it's a great way to get kids to eat lots of different stuff, and I wanted to put it out there for anyone stuck in sandwich-and-an-apple bag lunch ruts. It's definitely worth the investment in a lunch container for this.

DAD TIP

If a container of rice is too boring, tinker with the little rice blob as much as you like. Sometimes I pat the rice into a firm square on a cutting board and then cut with a cookie cutter. Lifted gently with a spatula, the rice takes and keeps a good shape if packed tightly. Or you can use your veggies to make a little face or monster. The options are endless here. Let your sous chef explore and have fun, while you just keep those healthy ingredients coming.

CHICKEN TORTILLA POPS

DIFFICULTY: Easy • **MAKES:** About 6 pops

If your child can roll play dough, he can do this. Easy. Don't tell the kiddos, but this is one of those things they'll make and exclaim, "Oh, wow, so cool!" and you'll think, "You're just rolling stuff. But whatever, eat up, Buttercup." I use chicken and cheese, but obviously feel free to switch it up with lunchmeats you like best. But take note: Rolling stuff into "pops" has a way of getting kids to eat things they might otherwise ignore, so maybe try a veggie they've shied away from in the past. Asparagus is great for rolling, as is spinach.

Here's what you need:

TOOLS
❏ 6 bamboo skewers, knife, cutting board

INGREDIENTS
❏ 1 soft tortilla

❏ 1 slice chicken lunchmeat

❏ 1 or 2 slices cheese

Here's what you do:

1 Put the tortilla down. Put the chicken on it. Put the cheese on top of the chicken. (If you're using a vegetable, throw it on last on the side, not the middle.)

2 Now, roll. The trick here is you're going for tightness. Roll firmly but gently so you don't bust the tortilla. If you or the kid needs to re-roll, no bigs.

3 Before you cut these things into individual pops, go ahead and stick in 6 skewers. Start where the flap unrolls and push the skewer through the flap and into the roll. Keep pushing until the tip emerges, just barely, on the other side. You can then pull it back in. But you want the whole thing to be supported, so I like to go all the way through. (If you're concerned about the sharp end poking the kids, I can't help you. It may happen. They'll be fine. Probably.)

4 Repeat the skewering along the flap every inch or so. Now you have a weird tortilla log with skewers in it. Awesome.

5 Slice between the skewers and boom! You've got individual pops. Stick the other ends in an apple for support—and a great side dish—or just go to town on them as is.

THE HONEA BOY SANDWICH

Contributed by Whit Honea

DIFFICULTY: Easy or medium, depending on knife skills

MAKES: 1 insanely big, delicious sandwich

My good friend Whit Honea is probably one of the best word jockeys I know. His blog, *The Honea Express* (*www.whithonea.com*), chronicles his adventures as a dad to two boys, Atticus and Zane. His writing is lyrical and hilarious and melancholy all at the same time—all of the feelings that encapsulate parenting. He is also the author of *The Parents' Phrase Book*, which I keep on hand as a sort of parenting bible when weird or potentially sticky situations or conversations come up. It's an invaluable resource from a parenting expert who offers funny, no-nonsense advice from someone who's been there, done that.

I'm incredibly pleased and proud to offer this family recipe, which officially puts the Dagwood on notice as best. sandwich. ever.

Here's Whit on the making of a family favorite:

It started with two boys and a dream. Also, bread.

We were in a popular chain restaurant, a sandwich shop, the kind where the kids walk down the line and say "Yes, please" to this and "No, thank you" to that while smearing their wet noses generously across the finger-stained glass—the kind of place that is generally followed by flu shots for dessert.

The boys each created strikingly similar sandwiches, and I couldn't help but wonder why I was paying so much for such simplicity, especially since we had all of their preferred ingredients rotting away in our pantry at home. That was the day the Honea Boy was born, and it weighed no pounds and however many ounces, depending on the cheese count. (I've never actually weighed a sandwich.)

Over the years we have experimented with a few variations, but there are some must-have staples for any version to be considered a Honea Boy and I have shared them all here.

Here's what you need:

TOOLS
❑ Knife, cutting board, toaster, utensils for spreading

INGREDIENTS
❑ Bread (We always use bread when we make a sandwich, usually 2 pieces, although I've seen it done with 3, which was amazing. These days we usually go with an Asiago bagel sliced in half (lengthwise) and gently toasted.)

Main Ingredients
❑ Lettuce of choice

❑ Hand-picked black olives

Toppings
❑ Red onion

❑ Sweet peppers

❑ Chili peppers

❑ Avocado

❑ Tomato

❑ Slice of cheese (Cheddar or Swiss are our favorites)

❑ Love

Sauces
❑ Mayonnaise

❑ Mustard

❑ Sriracha sauce

Here's what you do:

1. Start with the prep work: Chop lettuce. Slice olives, onions, peppers, avocado, and tomato. Slice the cheese.

2. Toast bread if desired, which it totally is.

3. Place toasted bread slices side by side on a plate, platter, or napkin.

4. Spread mayonnaise and any additional sauces you like on the bread.

5. Place cheese just so.

6. Arrange olives and lettuce in the biggest pile possible while carefully straddling the line between sandwich and salad.

7. Add additional topping(s) to taste. Top with the other piece of bread.

One of my favorite memories of my daughter making food all by herself happened on a lazy weekday after school. I had just finished a workout and needed to shower. Emme was either reading or playing, I forget. I popped out of the shower and headed to the kitchen to prepare her a snack, and there she was at the table, gobbling up apple slices slathered in sugar and cinnamon. She had made Apple Pie in a Bag all by herself, and I couldn't have been prouder. As someone who learned to handle frying pans and master hot ovens by myself at an early age, I knew she was on the right track.

Because all snack times are different—sometimes you need a healthy filler before more playground time and sometimes you just crave a gooey, chocolate-y mess of whatever—I tried to offer a wide spectrum of choices. From DIY trail mix (GORP—Good Ol' Raisins and Peanuts) to Cucumber Tea Party Sandwiches, I'm sure you'll find something in here for any between-meal occasion.

AGUA FRESCA

DIFFICULTY: Easy • **MAKES:** 3–4 tall glasses

We live close to the Mission neighborhood in San Francisco, and one of our favorite treats comes from one of the best taquerias. On a hot day, there's nothing quite like a cantaloupe agua fresca to cool you down. Translated as "fresh water," these are made with only a few simple ingredients: fresh fruit, water, and sugar. We've had watermelon, mango, pineapple, strawberry—you name it. But our favorite is cantaloupe. It's cool and sweet and earthy—just the thing for a quick afternoon pick-me-up. Plus, at home, you can monitor the sugar content.

Here's what you need:

TOOLS

❏ Knife, cutting board, blender, tall glasses, strainer (optional)

INGREDIENTS

❏ 1 whole cantaloupe

❏ 1½ cups water

❏ 2–4 tablespoons sugar

❏ Ice, limes, mint (all optional)

Here's what you do:

1 Cut up the cantaloupe into chunks.

2 Add the chunks into your blender, along with the water and 2 tablespoons of sugar. Blend until smooth. That's it. Starting with the smaller amount of sugar allows you to keep adding until you make the drink just sweet enough but not *so* sweet that the kids are bouncing off the walls.

DAD TIP

These instructions are the super easy way that any kid can do in about 5 to 10 minutes. The more traditional way involves blending just the fruit first, and then pressing the pulp into a strainer over a pitcher until the pitcher fills with just juice. Then, you add the water and sugar to the pitcher, stir, and you're done. It takes longer, and I happen to like a little pulp in my drinks, so I usually go with the easier route. I also like to add mint or basil to the blender for an even tastier treat with herbal notes. Tinker around with sugar and water and herb levels until you get yours just how you like it.

BLOWTORCH MARSHMALLOWS

This is a great way to dress up ordinary hot chocolate into something your little ones will remember forever. Emme and I gave this a try when we were caramelizing marshmallows in the microwave for another book I wrote (*Dad's Book of Awesome Science Experiments*) and decided this was a top-notch way to make the perfect garnish for hot chocolate. It involves the use of a kitchen torch, but you can easily just put the marshmallows on a skewer or fork and use the gas stove instead.

Here's what you need:

TOOLS
❏ Kitchen torch (microwave for safer option), plate

INGREDIENTS
❏ Big marshmallows!

❏ Hot chocolate

Here's what you do:

1 It's simple. Put as many marshmallows as you'd like to toast on a plate. Spread them out. Give them room.

2 Now take your kitchen torch and flame 'em up. Doesn't really matter if you burn them or they start to flame up. Just blow them out. Let your sous chef hold the torch, if you think she's ready. Kids get a big kick out of this, as if they're doing something dangerous and illicit.

3 Add toasted marshmallows to your favorite hot chocolate, or just eat as is.

4 If you don't have a torch or don't feel like handing a flame thrower to the children (but you should), just put a couple of marshmallows on a plate and slip it into the microwave for 15 seconds or so. They'll puff up at first and then fall flat, cooking until dark and golden. The more you "burn" them, the more they become caramelly and almost salty. Scrape off the plate and add to hot chocolate for a toasted marshmallow treat any time.

GORP (GOOD OL' RAISINS AND PEANUTS)

DIFFICULTY: Easy • **MAKES:** 8 servings

I'll always remember the first time I had GORP. I was in Maine with my aunt and uncle for the summer and we planned to hike up one of the presidential peaks in the White Mountains. We had our gear, our boots, our bags all ready to go. And there's my uncle at the counter mixing up peanuts and raisins and M&M's. What, I asked, was he doing? He filled me in on an age-old hiking tradition that I continue to this day with my own family. It's a perfect way to get kids excited about mixing ingredients and involves no cooking whatsoever. The youngest of your kitchen helpers can do this, and then enjoy the benefits of his dish in the great outdoors.

Here's what you need:

TOOLS

❏ Bowl, measuring cup, large spoon, large plastic bag or airtight container

INGREDIENTS

❏ 1 cup peanuts (or almonds)

❏ ¼ cup raisins (or dried cranberries or other fruit—you get the idea. Ingredients are up to your helper's taste.)

❏ ¼ cup chocolate chips or M&M's

Here's what you do:

1 This is always so fun to make and it's super fast. Just have your helper dump the peanuts, raisins, and chocolate chips into the bowl. Stir. Done! Store in an airtight container or bag, then dole out a handful before a hike.

2 Feel free to customize. Try dried pineapple and mango pieces for a tropical theme or dried cranberries and pumpkin seeds for a fall theme. Let your kids have fun.

DAD TIP

If you're using this just as an after-school snack, it doesn't matter what kind of chocolate you use. If you plan on actually hiking with it, try M&M's instead. On hot days, they won't melt like chocolate chips and create a big gooey mess every time you reach for a handful.

CUCUMBER TEA PARTY SANDWICHES

DIFFICULTY: Easy

MAKES: 1 sandwich cut up into 2 triangles. Or 4 triangles. Who knows? Go crazy

Sometimes your kids really want to throw a tea party. I get it. They're awesome—even the pretend ones where you have to sit there and sip ever so daintily on air in plastic cups. Mmm. Fun times. But if you really want to put some fancy in the party, a few simple cucumber sandwiches never fail to do the trick. They take all of 5 minutes, taste delicate and clean, and will put a sure smile on kids' faces because they're eating real food at the tea party. Plus, they can do it all by themselves while you kick back with a fresh pot of make-believe's best brew.

Here's what you need:

TOOLS
❑ Knife, cutting board

INGREDIENTS
❑ 2 slices white bread

❑ 1 tablespoon whipped cream cheese

❑ ¼ cucumber

Here's what you do:

1 Grab one of your slices of bread and slather it with a thin layer of cream cheese. You can buy whipped cream cheese now, and I find this is light and airy and spreads really well.

2 Slice your cucumber into thin circles. Again, let your sous chef take the lead while you put on an appropriate tea party outfit.

3 Layer a few circles on your cream cheese so that everything is nice and even, and then stack the next layer of bread on top to complete the sandwich.

4 Here's what makes it fancy: cutting. Have the kiddo slice off all the crusts and then cut diagonally so she has 2 triangles. You can go bonkers and let her keep slicing and dicing until you have a plateful of tiny triangles if you'd like. Up to you. Or her. Or him. Tea parties have never been so real-life tasty.

NACHO TOWER OF DOOM

DIFFICULTY: Easy • **MAKES:** 1 plate of delicious nachos

My wife came up with this, and I can't thank her enough. It's become a go-to family snack and, sometimes, meal. If you make traditional nachos (a pile of chips topped with cheese), you always end up with chips on the bottom that have no topping. And chips with no topping are the *worst*. But by individually inserting each chip into a slurry of bean and cheese you can ensure that each chip has some good stuff attached to it. Don't underestimate the power of a perfectly topped nacho. Come on, I'll show you what I mean.

Here's what you need:

TOOLS

❏ Oven, oven mitts, cheese grater, can opener, oven-safe plate (most ceramic plates are OK), fork

INGREDIENTS

❏ Cheddar cheese, to grate into ¼–½ cup

❏ ½ can black beans

❏ Big handful of tortilla chips

❏ Sour cream, salsa, guacamole—all optional but not really

Here's what you do:

1 First, preheat the oven to 350°F.

2 Next, grate your cheese. I like to add a whole bunch multiple times over the course of this recipe, but I realize some people aren't so into cheese. So grate anywhere from ¼ cup to ½ cup to meet your personal preferences.

3 Open a can of black beans, drain liquid, and dump about ¼ cup right onto an oven-proof plate. Mush them up with a fork. They don't have to be beaten into a pulp. Just enough to mush each one, and by all means, leave some unmushed if you like. But the mushier you make them, the easier it will be to stand the nachos up.

4 Sprinkle a layer of cheese in the bean mush and stir around. You should have a rough paste.

5 Now the magic happens. Take your chips and stand them up in your bean and cheese mulch. Just gently press any edge into place, starting in the center and going out until the plate is filled with endless nachos, pointing into the air.

6 Once you're good with your miniature Nacho Stonehenge, sprinkle on the rest of your cheese. Cover nachos. And beans. And the plate.

7 Then stick in oven. You don't really have to *cook* anything here. You're just melting the cheese and heating up the beans. So 5 to 7 minutes should do the trick.

8 Be careful when you remove from the oven. The plate will be hot, but give it a few minutes and it will cool. Add sour cream, salsa, or guacamole on top or on the side. Whatever you like. It's your nacho creation.

DAD TIP

We like to put pillows on our laps and put the plate on our pillow while watching a good show. Such a fun snack deserves a fun presentation.

MICROWAVE S'MORES

DIFFICULTY: Easy • **MAKES:** 1 s'more

I don't know if anything says summer evenings like a s'more. Chocolate, toasted marshmallow, graham crackers . . . the flavor combination always brings me back to Northern Michigan. A lake. A campfire. Relatives gathered around and gobbling up treats. Even the youngest kids can work a skewer over the fire with a little teaching or help, and then make their very own dessert sandwich. Thankfully, you don't need a lake and a campfire to do this on the fly. If you have a microwave and all the ingredients, you're good to go. This is a great sleepover hit that little chefs can prepare for themselves. And by all means, try a variety of types of chocolate. We've found that caramel- or mint-filled chocolates add another dimension of deliciousness.

Here's what you need:

TOOLS
❏ Microwave, plate

INGREDIENTS
❏ 2 graham cracker squares

❏ 1 chocolate bar square

❏ 1 large marshmallow

Here's what you do:

1 Put 1 of your crackers on the plate and top with the chocolate and then the marshmallow. Still with me? Good. Almost done. Seriously, it's that easy.

2 Now toss in the microwave and power it up for about 15 seconds. You can watch the marshmallow puff up. Once it's puffy, that means all the internal steam is cooking. Yay. Done. By all means, you can keep cooking until it becomes caramelly brown and volcano hot. But if you want to eat these right away, just a little puffiness should do the trick.

3 Remove from microwave, top with second graham cracker square. Close your eyes and envision yourself on a lake, and enjoy.

BAKED BAGEL CHIPS

DIFFICULTY: Medium • **MAKES:** 20–24 chips, if you use 3–4 leftover bagels

What do you do with hard, day-old bagels that no one wants to eat? Make them even *harder*, of course. Then they'll eat them like crazy. Trust me, it makes sense. This is a great way to zap a new use into food you might otherwise throw out, offering the kiddos a lesson in using what you have and wasting as little as possible. Plus, they taste pretty dang good.

Here's what you need:

TOOLS

❏ Oven, serrated knife, cutting board, cookie sheet, oven mitts

INGREDIENTS

❏ 3–4 day-old bagels (not moldy; just not great for eating like a regular bagel)

❏ Pinch of coarse salt

Here's what you do:

1 Preheat the oven to 350°F.

2 Slice the bagels into thin circles, like big circular chips, about ¼" thick. Don't worry if they don't look perfect. Bagels are generally easy to slice through, so this is a good one to teach knife skills to kids who are ready. Let the serrated blade do the cutting, while you add a little force. You can cut them into smaller pieces at this point or keep big. Up to you.

3 Layer the slices on a cookie sheet and bake for about 10–12 minutes, or until lightly brown and crispy. If you want them even crispier, cook for longer. Just make sure they don't start to darken too much. There's a fine line between crispy and yucky.

4 Remove from oven and, if you want, sprinkle with a dash of coarse salt. Kosher salt works great. Once cooled, store in a plastic bag or airtight container.

HOWLING GOOD HUMMUS WITH RAINBOW STICKS

DIFFICULTY: Medium • **MAKES:** 4 servings

This is one of those recipes you'll make and then think, "I can't believe I ever bought this stuff pre-made." It's fast, easy, and oh so good. It's also a super healthy snack chock-full of protein for little athletes. So there's that, too. As for the veggies, you're basically making a chilled dish of crudité—an assortment of colorful and delicious vegetables. It's not rocket science—you're basically slicing and dicing—but this is a great recipe for teaching knife skills and how to attack vegetables and turn them into ready-to-eat snacks. Go slow, have fun, and get ready to dip.

Here's what you need:

TOOLS

❑ Food processor, strainer, large bowl, small bowl, measuring cup and spoons, stirring spoon, knife, cutting board, serving platter

INGREDIENTS

Hummus

❑ 1 (15-ounce) can chickpeas

❑ 1 lemon

❑ ¼ cup tahini

❑ Salt to taste

❑ 1 garlic clove, minced

❑ 1 dash cumin

❑ 2 tablespoons olive oil, plus a little more for drizzling on top

❑ 1 dash paprika for garnish

Rainbow Sticks

❑ 1 carrot

❑ 1 red pepper

❑ 1 yellow pepper

❑ 1 orange pepper

❑ 1 cucumber

❑ ½ jicama

❑ 10 green beans

❑ 1 celery stalk

Here's what you do to make the hummus:

1. Open the can of chickpeas and pour into a strainer over a bowl to retain the liquid. It comes in handy later when you're trying to get the consistency just right. Squeeze a big lemon into a small bowl and remove any seeds that came out.

2. Set aside the chickpeas for a moment and add tahini, salt, minced garlic, cumin, and lemon juice into processor. Blend for about a minute until smooth. Scrape sides with spoon and blend for a few more seconds.

3. Now, add half of your chickpeas and the oil and then blend until smooth. Add the other half and blend some more. Stop from time to time to scrape the sides.

4. If it feels too thick, add a few tablespoons of the drained chickpea water. Add 1 spoonful at a time and blend until smooth.

5. Scoop out a nice portion and flatten a little bit. Drizzle in a touch of oil and then sprinkle some paprika over top for garnish and added flavor. Serve with chips or veggies. Store the rest in the fridge in an airtight container for a week or so.

Here's what you do to make the rainbow sticks:

1. The ingredient list is long, but don't be intimidated. Just buy what you think the kids will eat—plus one or two. Adventure is good for everyone.

2. Wash everything.

3. Next, it's time to slice and dice. Again, let the kids take the lead while you monitor—or grab a newspaper and chill out, depending on their skill level. Chop off the ends of the carrots and then cut in half lengthwise. Put flat part down and cut long strips. For the peppers, cut off the tops and then remove seeds and innards. Slice away. You can either cut cucumber wheels or sticks, depending on your preference. Jicama is always tricky as it's big and hard, so be careful with any slipping knives. Green beans—cut off the ends. Celery you can slice like carrots almost.

4. The great thing about this recipe is that it teaches kids cutting skills and arranging. Try having them set up rainbows of peppers and carrots, bordered by the green beans and celery stalks. But you'll be surprised at the direction this dish takes with chef trainees at the helm. Let them go wild and make their own design. Add a bowl of the hummus and you're off and eating.

PARMESAN PITA CHIPS

DIFFICULTY: Medium • **MAKES:** About 4 dozen chips

Like a bagel chip, this recipe calls for turning day-old baked goods into something new and wonderful instead of just throwing them out. I like the reuse factor and the idea of doing something creative with regular ol' products. They're just as tasty as store-bought pita chips, without any preservatives or additives. Serve them with cut carrots and a side of Minty Pea Dip (see recipe in this chapter) or hummus and you're good to go.

Here's what you need:

TOOLS

❏ Oven, oven mitts, cookie sheet, pizza cutter, measuring cups and spoons, bowl, cooking brush, big spoon

INGREDIENTS

❏ 4 pieces pita bread

❏ ½ cup grated Parmesan cheese

❏ 1½ tablespoons sesame seeds

❏ 6 tablespoons olive oil

Here's what you do:

1 Preheat the oven to 425°F.

2 Split each pita bread in half—they are usually pre-cut and ready for this—and then use the pizza cutter to cut each half into 3 wedges. Peel open and cut again at the pita seam so you now have 6 triangles for each half. They're thinner this way and cook up crispier. Place wedges on cookie sheet.

3 In a bowl, combine cheese and seeds. (Or just cheese if you like, or nothing at all! This is worth doing several ways to find your favorite.)

4 Brush the top of each pita wedge with oil and sprinkle the cheese and seed mixture on each slice.

5 Bake for 5 to 10 minutes, or until light brown and a little crispy. Store in bags when cool or another airtight container. These make a great pre-sport snack for your little athletes, or just a fun dipping snack with hummus.

MANGO HEDGEHOGS

DIFFICULTY: Easy • **MAKES:** 2 hedgehogs

There are numerous ways to slice mangoes, but this is a sure-fire way to make something fun and inviting. Kids love to smash their faces into these, and why not? Let them do the cutting, the popping, and the eating. It's a great after-school or anytime snack that requires no cooking.

Here's what you need:

TOOLS
❏ Knife, cutting board

INGREDIENTS
❏ 1 ripe mango

❏ 1 lime wedge, 1 sprig mint, 1 dash chili powder (all optional)

DAD TIP

If you'd like, squeeze a little lime juice onto the hog and add a few rough cuts of mint. This makes a super hairy hedgehog while adding to the deliciousness of ripe fruit. If your kid likes hot stuff, a few dashes of chili powder make a great Mexican street food–style treat.

Here's what you do:

1 Take a look at your mango. It's sort of this weird, large oval. Turn it so you can see two sides that sort of plump out. These are the sides you want to slice off. Just go from top to bottom, carving off a big lump from each side.

2 Now, working with one lump at a time, slice 4 lines through the mango flesh, being sure to go deep enough to cut through the fruit but *not* deep enough to pierce the skin. Now, repeat 4 times going across the lines you just made. You should now have a mango lump that looks as if it's ready for cubing.

3 Here comes the cool part. Grab the mango lump in both hands so your fingers are on the sides and your thumbs are on the skin. Push your thumbs until all those cube slices "pop" out, forming your little hedgehog. (For mango salsa or other mango dishes, this is a great way to slice off perfect cubes, by the way.) Repeat with the other lump. Done and done. Kids can pluck off the cubes, or just stick their faces into the inside-out mango.

MINTY PEA DIP

DIFFICULTY: Easy • **MAKES:** 2 cups

This one comes straight from a trip to London and a plate loaded with fish and chips. On the side, the restaurant served a traditional English favorite of mushy peas—sweet, delicious mashed-up peas. They were a light counterpoint to the heavy fried fish, and I knew right away that with a few additions, they'd become the perfect dip alternative to hummus or guacamole. It's easy to make and goes just great with pita chips or as a side on its own.

Here's what you need:

TOOLS
- ❏ Food processor, serving bowls, measuring spoons

INGREDIENTS
- ❏ 1 (12-ounce) bag of frozen peas, defrosted (Or fresh if you can find them. They're fun to peel.)
- ❏ 2 tablespoons olive oil
- ❏ 10–12 sprigs of mint
- ❏ Salt and pepper to taste

Here's what you do:

1 Make sure you defrost and drain the peas. They should be room temperature. Stick a package in the fridge overnight and then let sit out for an hour or so before starting. Even better, use fresh peas because they're fun to peel and eat straight from the pod. But I realize it's not springtime all the time.

2 When the peas are ready, add to your food processor. Drizzle in oil and add mint leaves—the more the mintier, so do this to your own taste. Ten to 12 leaves is a good starting point. Add salt and pepper.

3 Now that everything's in . . . chop! You don't want it to become too pasty and smooth, though, so a few rough chops will get the job done just right. Use a spoon to scoop goop off the sides. Even if a few peas remain whole or mostly whole, that's fine. You want some mouthfeel to the dip.

4 When you're satisfied with the mint amount (you can always add more after a quick taste) and the consistency, spoon into bowls and serve with chips. This is a refreshing, healthy dip for all occasions.

CRAZY DELICIOUS CARAMEL CORN

DIFFICULTY: Hard • **MAKES:** About 6 cups

This recipe is at once crazy delicious and scary as all get-out. As much as I enjoy caramel, it's nerve-wracking to make it—especially with a little sous chef nearby. So you be the judge on just how much your kids can do when it comes to handling molten sugar. I like to take the lead on that part, while my helper does the rest. In the end, you're still going to have a fun treat that is just perfect for a lazy fall day. Or, even better, a baseball game on TV.

Here's what you need:

TOOLS

❏ Oven, cookie sheet, oven mitts, large mixing bowl, spoon, measuring cups and spoons, medium saucepan

INGREDIENTS

❏ Cooking spray

❏ 1 (3½-ounce) bag of plain microwave popcorn, popped

❏ 1 cup brown sugar

❏ ½ cup (1 stick) butter

❏ ½ cup corn syrup

❏ Dash of salt

❏ 1 cup dry-roasted, salted peanuts

Here's what you do:

1 Preheat the oven to 200°F and spray your cookie sheet with oil. Then pop your popcorn.

2 In a medium saucepan, combine brown sugar, butter, syrup, and salt. Cook on medium-high heat for about 5 minutes—until everything is melted and smooth. Stir constantly and watch for popping bubbles that fly through the air and get on your hands. There's always a fine line between teaching great cooking skills and being safe. Burning sugar is no joke, but you also don't want to freak out your little sous chef to the point that she's afraid to try the recipe, so try not to overdo the warnings. And yet, be careful. . . .

3 In a large bowl, combine popcorn and nuts. Then add your caramel sauce. Mix well.

4 When everything is mixed, it should cool down a bit. Use your spoon to spread a thin layer on the cookie sheet.

5 Bake for about an hour, stirring every 15 minutes or so. The baking at low heat is what gives it a nice crunch, so take your time. Then, enjoy.

GUACAMOLE

DIFFICULTY: Medium • **MAKES:** 1 cup

I'll always remember when I first learned how to cut an avocado. I was at a friend's house, and his mom asked me to get an avocado ready for dinner. I sliced and diced and peeled and turned the delicate little fruit into a project right out of Hannibal Lecter's crime book. It was a mess. Then his mom showed me how to slice around the entire thing until I had two halves. Whack the knife into the seed, twist, pull . . . voila! Two perfect, ready-to-eat avocados. This is a great recipe for teaching knife skills on one of the world's best fruits.

Here's what you need:

TOOLS

❏ Knife, cutting board, mixing bowl, measuring spoons, fork

INGREDIENTS

❏ 2 avocados

❏ ¼ jalapeño pepper, super fresh and green

❏ 1 teaspoon olive oil

❏ 1 lime

❏ Coarse salt to taste

❏ Pepper to taste

Here's what you do:

1 First, cut your avocados and dump pieces into bowl. You're going to use a fork to mash everything around, so it doesn't matter what they look like.

2 Next, chop up your pepper into diced bits. I find that jalapeño adds a fresh heat that can't be mimicked with dried pepper flakes. Your call on whether it works for your family. (Worth a try, though, or use a hot sauce in small doses to start.)

3 Add pepper to bowl and drizzle in the oil. Cut lime in half and squeeze juice into bowl. Here's a tip: Before cutting limes, roll them hard against a hard surface to release extra juice inside. Yum.

4 Sprinkle with a healthy amount of coarse salt and then some pepper, and then use your fork to mash everything together. I like chunkier guacamole, so I don't go overboard. But some people like it smooth, so do what works for you. Serve with a side of tortilla chips or as a topping or filling for tacos and burritos.

MEXICAN STREET FOOD FRUIT SKEWERS

DIFFICULTY: Easy • **MAKES:** 8 skewers

On a hot day in San Francisco's Mission District, you can find cart vendors hawking lineups of ripe, sweet fruit on enormous skewers—pineapple, mango, watermelon. They're delicious and ready to eat as is . . . or you can make them even better by adding a touch of salt, some lime, and just the right amount of chili powder. Let your sous chef personalize these any way he wants.

Here's what you need:

TOOLS

❑ Knife, cutting board, 8 long bamboo skewers, measuring spoons

INGREDIENTS

❑ 1 watermelon

❑ 1 pineapple

❑ 1 cucumber

❑ 1 jicama

❑ 1 mango

❑ 1 lime

❑ 1 teaspoon coarse salt

❑ ½ teaspoon chili powder

Here's what you do:

1 I'll show you how to make a pineapple-only skewer. Slice the pineapple until you have about 8 long, thickish slices and then run a skewer end to end.

2 Ready for the hard part? Cut the lime and squeeze it onto the fruit. You don't have to go bonkers. Just a nice coat. Then add sprinkles of salt and chili powder to taste. Use a lot if you like the heat or just try a dash if you want to start slow.

PERSONALIZED POPCORN BAGS

DIFFICULTY: Super easy • **MAKES:** 2 popcorn bags

So consider this a starter recipe for even the smallest of sous chefs. It's so easy it feels almost like cheating—like the Sandra Lee of child's cookery. But man, kids go bonkers for these things. You can flavor the popcorn any way you want—salt and pepper, butter, chili powder, garlic powder, grated cheese, you name it. But the fun comes from taking an ordinary paper lunch sack and personalizing it. The kids always feel like it's their very own special snack they made. And, well, it *is*.

Here's what you need:

TOOLS

❑ Microwave, paper lunch bags, crayons, grater or microplane, measuring spoon

INGREDIENTS

❑ 1 microwave popcorn bag

❑ 1 stick cold butter

❑ Salt, pepper, or other seasonings, to taste

Here's what you do:

1 Give the kids paper lunch bags and crayons and let them go to town on the decorating.

2 Stick a bag of microwave popcorn into the machine and let it pop.

3 If your sous chef is ready, have her do this next part. Take the stick of butter and grate it over a cheese grater or microplane. You don't need much—½ tablespoon is perfect. Grating it thin makes the butter easier to spread around and melt.

4 When the popcorn is done, remove from microwave and divide into the paper bags. Add butter, salt, and pepper, then fold the top closed and shake. This is a great snack for on the go.

WATERMELON LIGHT SABERS

DIFFICULTY: Easy • **MAKES:** 8–10 sabers

Like so many easy recipes kids love, this one is all in the cutting. In the end, you're going to have a whole bunch of watermelon light sabers that are sweet and salty and just right for a summer day. Yes, it's just a different form of your traditional watermelon wedge, but little chefs love to make these. And fight with them. And then, of course, gobble them up.

Here's what you need:

TOOLS
- ❏ Knife, cutting board, serving plate

INGREDIENTS
- ❏ 1 medium watermelon
- ❏ 1 teaspoon coarse salt

Here's what you do:

1 Start in the center of the watermelon and slice off 4 circles about 1" thick each. Store the rest of your watermelon.

2 Lay the circles flat on the cutting board and slice so you have 4 or 5 sticks. Cut off the rind from one end of each stick, leaving one end with the rind intact. If the sticks are big, be careful when you move them to a serving plate, as they can break apart.

3 Sprinkle with a dash of salt and prepare for one delicious battle.

CHEESY CORN WHEELS

DIFFICULTY: Medium • **MAKES:** 8 wheels

Want to get kids stoked about cooking? Give them a few corn "wheels" and let them make tracks in a make-believe snowscape of crumbled feta and mint. Not only is this ridiculously fun to do, it's incredibly delicious and good for you. Kids, however, won't be able to get enough of rolling their wheels through the "snow." It'll be messy, sure, but it's worth it. Bigtime.

Here's what you need:

TOOLS

❑ Stove, pot, knife, cutting board, tongs or strainer

INGREDIENTS

❑ 4 cups water

❑ 2 ears of corn, shucked

❑ 2 sprigs mint

❑ ½ cup feta cheese

Here's what you do:

1 Preheat a pot of water to boiling while your sous chef shucks the corn.

2 Cook the corn in the water for about 5 minutes. Corn is sweet and delicious barely cooked or even raw—you don't need to boil it into oblivion.

3 While the corn is cooking, chop the mint and crumble the feta. Now spread it all over the cutting board. It should look like a canvas of mint and feta. Mmmm.

4 When the corn is ready, remove from the water and let dry. Now, chop up each ear into circles, so that you have 8 or so wheels, or about 4 from each ear.

5 Now have the kiddos roll the wheels all over the cheese and mint layer, making tracks and letting the kernels soak up all that deliciousness. This is a great snack or even a side dish for any meal. Sprinkle with pepper if you like, but I avoid salt, as the cheese is super salty enough.

PROSCIUTTO MELON BALLS

DIFFICULTY: Easy • **MAKES:** 2 dozen balls

Nothing brings me back to Italy like a tabletop picnic of the salty-sweet combination of fruits and meats. This became a favorite go-to hiking meal while traveling, and I like to replicate it at home because it's easy and tastes so darn good. The combination of ripe, sweet fruit and soft, salty meat . . . mmm, irresistible. This makes for an easy, awesome dish that a skilled sous chef can do on her own while you focus on a main course. It's also a great assembly line recipe if you have a bunch of kids eager to help.

Here's what you need:

TOOLS

❑ Knife, cutting board, spoon, melon baller, serving platter, toothpicks

INGREDIENTS

❑ 1 ripe cantaloupe

❑ 4–6 slices prosciutto

Here's what you do:

1 First, slice the cantaloupe in half. Now, scoop out the innards and seeds into the sink or compost bin.

2 This is the fun part. Take the melon baller and scoop out as many balls as you can. Toss them on the platter, being careful not to eat them all. (This is a problem with ripe fruit. . . .)

3 When you have a bunch of balls ready to go, tear off a piece of prosciutto and do your best to wraps the balls. They don't have to be perfect and they won't look it—believe me. So long as the meat covers the fruit, you're good to go. If you want to ensure the meat stays on, insert a toothpick through the meat and into the fruit. (Remember my philosophy that kids will eat anything on a stick.)

4 At this point, you can just roll the meat-covered balls back onto the platter. Make as many as you can and enjoy.

PEANUT BUTTERY CHIP MUFFINS

DIFFICULTY: Medium • **MAKES:** 1 dozen muffins

I absolutely love peanut butter—it tastes wonderful, it's got great fats, and it's loaded with protein. And it's the leading example in one of those Got Milk? commercials. Milk and peanut butter go hand in hand for me. This recipe is creamy, muffin-y, and just the perfect amount of peanut buttery. If the ingredients leave you feeling like you're on peanut butter overload, substitute peanut butter chips with chocolate chips instead. Heck, try both.

Here's what you need:

TOOLS
- ❏ Oven, muffin pan, oven mitts, electric mixer, measuring cups and spoons, mixing bowls, spoons

INGREDIENTS
- ❏ Cooking spray
- ❏ 1 cup smooth peanut butter (no sugar or added junkola)
- ❏ 1 egg
- ❏ ¼ cup sugar
- ❏ ¼ cup brown sugar, packed
- ❏ 1 cup milk
- ❏ 1½ cups all-purpose flour
- ❏ 1 tablespoon baking powder
- ❏ ½ cup peanut butter chips

Here's what you do:

1. Preheat the oven to 375°F and grease muffin pan with your spray.

2. In a bowl, combine peanut butter, egg, both sugars, and milk, and then go to town on it with an electric mixer until smooth.

3. Stop mixing and have your sous chef add in the flour and baking powder. Start mixer on slow, otherwise you'll have a kitchen full of flour. Mix until just blended. Don't overmix.

4. Now manually stir in peanut butter chips. Pour or spoon batter into muffin pan so each cup is about ¾ full.

5. Bake for about 15 minutes, or until they're light brown on top. You can stick a knife in the middle to test. The knife should come out clean. Pour a tall glass of milk and enjoy.

APPLE PIE IN A BAG

DIFFICULTY: Easy • **MAKES:** 1 baggie of delight

Have you ever walked into a home where someone was making an apple pie? The smell is overwhelming. It's like a memory of fall and childhood coming back to hit you, every single time. Well, this is sort of like that—only more portable. Imagine whipping open your own bag of apple pie–smelling delight for snack time. That's how cool it is. I like turning the ordinary into something outrageously cool—that's exactly what this recipe is all about.

Here's what you need:

TOOLS
❏ Knife, cutting board, zip-top plastic bag

INGREDIENTS
❏ 1 apple

❏ 1 lemon

❏ 1 pinch sugar

❏ 1 pinch cinnamon

Here's what you do:

1 First things first: Have your sous chef cut the apple into wedges. Do the same with the lemon.

2 Toss the apple slices in a baggie and squeeze a bit of lemon on them. Seal bag and mix around. This prevents browning, just in case you're making these for eating later. You can skip this if you're eating the apples right away.

3 Next, open the bag and add 1 pinch of sugar and 1 pinch of cinnamon. I don't give exact amounts here only because I don't want to make you feel married to a certain amount. Apples are sweet enough as is. They certainly don't *need* sugar, but this is a fun-time snack so go ahead and add a tiny bit you're comfortable with. Add as much cinnamon as you like and then reseal, shake, and get ready to open a bag that smells like sweetness and fall and childhood.

ORANGE SNAILS

DIFFICULTY: Easy • **MAKES:** 1 snail

Ever wanted to create a whimsical little something for snack time or packed lunches? This is for you. All you need is one of those teeny tiny mandarin oranges and a good knife. (A pen also works great, but that's optional.) This is a fun afternoon snack-time activity to show kids that an ordinary orange can become something super cool with a few precise cuts. Plus, it just looks cute.

Here's what you need:

TOOLS
❑ Cutting board, paring knife, pen (optional)

INGREDIENTS
❑ Mandarin orange (Cuties)

Here's what you do:

1 So the trick to this is peeling the orange while leaving as much of the peel intact as possible. I like to start by removing the bit of peel where the stem connects at the top of the orange. Then I slice just through the peel from the top of the orange to the bottom (without cutting into the orange itself) and gently loosen the peel from the fruit until I can remove the orange, intact.

2 Here's the fun cutting part. Cut the orange peel into one long, wide strip—wide enough to hold the orange and long enough to reach about ¾ of the way around the orange. You'll be putting the orange on its side, like a wheel, inside of this wide, cupping strip of peel, to approximate a snail. Trim what will be the front end of the peel to make 2 short triangles that look like antennae.

3 When finished cutting, you can add the orange to the peel again. Feel free to add a little face with a pen and watch your sous chef delight in his new snack-time friend.

YOGURT FRUIT POPS

DIFFICULTY: Medium • **MAKES:** About 6 big ice pops or 12 small ones

I'm not a fan of hiding healthy stuff behind bad stuff, because then all of a sudden you have a kid who won't eat asparagus without having it soaked in batter, inserted into a Twinkie, fried, and then drizzled with chocolate and dipped in sugared honey jam marshmallow sauce. Yum, right? But with this? It's impossible not to hide the good stuff. It just gets whirred into a big, healthy mix of calcium-and-protein-rich yogurt and all of a sudden you're eating an amazing snack (or a great on-the-go breakfast). Healthy, delicious, sweet, good for you, and fun to make. My kind of recipe.

Here's what you need:

TOOLS

❑ Blender, knife, cutting board, measuring cups and spoons, ice pop molds if you have them (ice cube trays or plastic cups if you don't), toothpicks or wooden sticks, plastic cling wrap

INGREDIENTS

❑ 2 cups nonfat plain yogurt (I like Greek yogurt but kids sometimes don't like the tartness. Use what the kids like, but use plain, nonsugared stuff.)

❑ 10 ounces frozen strawberries

❑ Handful fresh or frozen blueberries

❑ 2 ounces milk

❑ 1–2 tablespoons honey, depending on how sweet you want it

Here's what you do:

1 This is as simple as tossing everything except the blueberries into the chopper. Yogurt, strawberries, milk, honey. Give that thing a whirl until the mix is evenly blended.

2 Now, if you have ice pop molds—they're easy to find in all manner of shapes nowadays and worth an investment if you make frozen treats a lot—layer a few blueberries on the bottom. Do the same for plastic cups or ice cube trays if that's what you're using.

3 Pour mixture on top of blueberries and add the stick end of your mold, or insert Popsicle sticks into cups or toothpicks into ice cube trays. If tilted Popsicle sticks or toothpicks drive you batty and you want them to stand up straight, just cover your cups or cubes with a layer of plastic wrap and then insert picks or sticks. The wrap keeps them in place.

4 Carefully slide your molds into the freezer and give them at least 3 or 4 hours. Overnight assures doneness.

DAD TIP

Feel free to tinker with this and come up with a recipe that suits your family perfectly. Some people enjoy bananas, while others enjoy better, more delicious fruit. Experiment away.

DINNER

5

Dinner in our house seems to go one of two ways: We somehow find ourselves with endless time and quickly fill it up with a ginormous family meal, or we're stuffing food into our faces as fast as possible on busy nights between soccer, school events, playtime, you name it.

I'm guessing your family's schedule is similar, so I tried to provide a good balance here between dishes you can make together on a busy weeknight and those you can take more time on during a lazy weekend day. In all of them, however, I urge you to work together—from picking out produce at the store or farmers' market to slicing it up for the finished product. Indeed, I know it can be slow going in the beginning at times, but just imagine how great it will be in a few years (yes, it takes time, so be patient) when you have a seasoned helper at your side to co-prepare the most delectable family meals. Stick with it and try to incorporate as much help and teamwork as possible into these dishes.

No matter which dishes you choose or how much help you have, it should be, at the end of the day, fun for all.

And, of course, delicious.

EASY BAKED TOMATO-GARLIC PASTA

DIFFICULTY: Medium • **MAKES:** 4–6 servings

I like this one because you have to work really, really hard to mess it up and not end up with something yummy for an easy weeknight dinner. Seriously, you would have to purposefully sabotage it to make people not like it. Even when it isn't cooked long enough or, say, hasn't got enough salt or oil, it's still pretty good. It's a wonderful starter entrée for your little sous chef. Made just right, it's insanely homey and rustic and delicious. Don't tell any guests, but it basically requires just throwing tomatoes into a baking dish and slathering on some oil.

Here's what you need:

TOOLS
❏ Oven, stove, baking dish, oven mitts, knife, cutting board, big spoon, large pot, strainer

INGREDIENTS
❏ Cherry tomatoes (1 or 2 bins, depending on how many people you're feeding)

❏ ½ cup olive oil

❏ Head of garlic

❏ Salt and pepper pinches

❏ Rosemary or any dry herb you like for tomatoes

❏ Pasta package of choice (we like spaghetti)

❏ Parmesan cheese

❏ Basil

Here's what you do:

1 Preheat oven to 400°F while you . . .

2 Wash and de-stem all your cherry tomatoes and then toss into your baking dish, which should be big enough to have only a single layer of tomatoes.

3 Now, dash in a whole mess of olive oil. Just spread it all around. (More oil means you're going to have a delicious oily sauce to layer on your pasta later, while less oil means you're going to have almost caramelized, sugary tomatoes. Some days I feel like absolutely drenching the tomatoes, but this recipe calls for just enough to give all the tomatoes a teeny tiny layer to bathe in.)

4 Remove cloves from garlic head and smash them on cutting board with flat part of knife. It's OK to crush them. Add those to the baking dish.

5 Once your ingredients are in, add salt and pepper—a few pinches of each. Add a little rosemary if you like—or any herb you like.

6 Mix ingredients with spoon to coat all the tomatoes and then stick in the oven.

7 Cook at 400°F for about 25–30 minutes, or until garlic is cooked. The tomatoes will be fine after 20 minutes or so, but biting into uncooked garlic is not so fun.

8 As your tomatoes cook, turn your attention to the pasta. Use any type you like and cook to the directions on the package—usually 10–11 minutes for dry spaghetti.

9 Once your tomatoes and garlic are done, remove from oven and spoon over drained spaghetti. Garnish with Parmesan cheese and top with basil if you'd like.

DAD TIP

We've also experimented with time and temperature on this one for different tastes and outcomes. Here's one awesome variation: Cook the tomatoes at about 250°F for a solid 3–4 hours. They become sugary, caramelized, almost burnt little bites of molten deliciousness. It's the perfect tweak for your little sous chef to master for a Sunday night family dinner.

SPAGHETTIPUS

DIFFICULTY: Medium • **MAKES:** 2 spaghettipi

You might have seen similar recipes to this online, probably imagined up by a genius in the kitchen. I tweaked it a tiny bit to make it easy for kids to do, but really you should probably do this on your own and surprise them with it. They will literally gasp with joy. It's all about the presentation. You take normal ingredients they've seen before, and then twist them up a bit for a happy surprise.

Here's what you need:

TOOLS

❑ Stove, large pot, knife, cutting board, tongs, bowl or serving dish

INGREDIENTS

❑ 1 hot dog

❑ 8 dry spaghetti strands

❑ 4 cups water

❑ Butter and cheese or sauce to serve (optional)

Here's what you do:

1. Boil water in your pot while you prepare the spaghettipi. Slice the hot dog in half.

2. Stand up your hot dog so the pointy end is on top. About an inch from the bottom, insert a spaghetti strand through the side of the dog until it goes all the way through and each half of the strand is even. Go slowly. If they break, no worries. Use another one. Repeat until each hot dog half has 4 spaghetti strands poking through it, creating 8 "legs" in all.

3. Now gently lower into pot of water and cook spaghetti according to its instructions—usually 9 to 11 minutes.

4. Remove from water with tongs, instead of straining, just to minimize any leg damage. At this point, the hot dog should be well boiled and the spaghetti just right. Each one should look like a perfect little octopus, with the pointy end as the "head" and the flatter, cut end as the rest of the body—complete with 8 legs dangling down. Use a knife to cut out 2 eyes and a smile on the top half of the hot dog, if you really want to impress. Just kind of gouge out two tiny circles for eyes and a half circle for the smile. It doesn't have to be perfect. You'll get better at it. Serve plain, or with butter and cheese or even in a "sea" of sauce in a bowl. No limits.

DIY ARZAK-ISH EGGS

DIFFICULTY: Hard • **MAKES:** 1 egg

This recipe comes straight from one of the world's greatest chefs—Juan Mari Arzak. I tried to make it as kid friendly as possible. Even though it's only a simple egg, it's a unique presentation. Kids will love to unwrap these little guys and serve atop a bed of rice or use in the Pickled Ginger Bibimbap recipe given later in this chapter. Although the ingredient list is short—egg, oil, salt, and pepper—the tool list is long. It takes a bit of work to get them ready and you have to watch the cooking time and method closely, but once you master it, you'll find these eggs are an easy way to make any dish sing. Thanks, Chef Arzak!

Here's what you need:

TOOLS

❑ Stove, large pot, plastic wrap, small bowls, butcher's twine, chopstick or large spoon (used to dangle egg into water), kitchen shears or scissors, towel

INGREDIENTS

❑ 1 teaspoon olive oil

❑ Pinch of salt

❑ Pinch of pepper

❑ 1 egg

Here's what you do:

1 Put water in a large pot and bring to a boil. You should have enough water in the pot to fully submerge the egg by at least an inch or so.

2 Take a large square of plastic wrap and place it gently over a small bowl so it covers the opening. It should be the size of, say, a piece of printer paper. You can always cut it later, so don't worry if it feels big.

3 Indent the wrap a tiny bit so you have a shallow bowl out of plastic wrap.

4 Add your oil into the teeny bowl of plastic wrap. Use your fingers to coat the entire plastic wrap bowl area. All this is great for sous chefs. Add a dash of salt and pepper to taste.

5 Next, gently crack your egg into the plastic wrap bowl. Make sure the yolk remains intact.

6 Gather up the sides of the plastic wrap and twist them together so that your shallow plastic wrap bowl looks like a sack filled with egg and oil. Join all the ends and twist together.

7 Cut off a foot-long piece of butcher twine and tie one end to the very top of the sack. Add a good knot of your choosing, as you just want to be sure the egg doesn't spill out. If you have a lot of excess plastic wrap twisting above the knot, cut it off.

8 Here's the cool part. Now that you have an egg sack wrapped up and dangling from a string, wrap the other end of the string around the chopstick a few times. You're going to put the chopstick over the pot and adjust the length of the string so that the egg sack dangles perfectly into the water. Give it a quick dunk to see if the egg sack dangles just right—it should be below the surface of the water but not touching the bottom, and adjust string once you find the right depth.

9 Once you have the perfect dangle height, tie off the string onto the chopstick, rest chopstick over the pot of boiling water, and let the cooking begin.

10 Cook for 4 minutes and 20 seconds. That's my preference. Four minutes seems like too little and anything else seems too long. But by all means, experiment. I like a firm egg white and a runny yolk, and I've found that 4 minutes and 20 seconds works great.

11 When it's ready, lift chopstick off pan and wipe off excess water from sack. Gently cut below the knot to unwrap the egg. It should be hot and fragile, so be careful not to slice through egg and release the yolk too soon. The end product should look like a nice puff of egg. Sometimes they even resemble flowers from all the plastic creases. Serve over rice or as a distinctive side to any meal.

PICKLED GINGER BIBIMBAP

DIFFICULTY: Medium to hard • **MAKES:** 2 big bowls

I like to cheat on this one using 90-second pouches of microwave rice. The dish timing can be tricky enough as it is, and this little cheat saves time and cleaning. Thanks to this miracle of microwave cookery, you and your little sous chef can whip up a semi-traditional Korean dish that is bright and colorful, sweet and spicy, hot and cold—everything you could ever want. It's a weeknight go-to that doesn't require any green side dishes because all the salad is mixed right in. I love that.

Here's what you need:

TOOLS

❏ Stove, frying pan with lid, knife, cutting board, 2 serving bowls

INGREDIENTS

❏ 1 small steak, about 4–6 ounces (or salmon or chicken—your call)

❏ ½ tablespoon butter or splash of oil

❏ ½ cup sliced red cabbage

❏ ¼ cup sliced carrots

❏ ¼ cup sliced cucumbers

❏ 1 pouch instant rice

❏ 2 eggs

❏ 1 big pinch pickled ginger

❏ 1 splash Sriracha hot sauce

Here's what you do:

1 To start, cook whatever protein you like in the frying pan. Emme enjoys salmon. I enjoy steak. I'm writing this, so I call steak. I like to grill it over medium heat in a splash of oil, while we prep the vegetables.

2 Prep the vegetables. You want julienne-style long, thin slices of everything. Let the sous chef go to town while you work on the protein. Or vice versa. Set the veggies aside in small piles.

3 These next steps require teamwork and quick action to plate. As the steak is coming to a finish, add rice pouch to microwave and cook. Just keep it in there after it's done cooking until you're ready to dump it into bowls.

4 The moment the steak is done, take it out of the pan and let it rest on the cutting board while you move on to the eggs. Crack 2 into a frying pan and follow the directions for the Simple Fried Egg (see recipe in Chapter 2). (Or, if you're feeling adventurous and have a great helper, use the DIY Arzak-ish Egg recipe earlier in this chapter.)

5 The eggs are your final ingredient to cook. When they're done, start adding everything to the bowls. Put in rice first, then add small piles of vegetables. Slice steak into thin slices and add veggies in small piles atop rice. Add a pinch of pickled ginger if you have it—it adds brightness and something sweet and spicy. Add a dash of hot sauce, and then add the whole cooked egg on top of everything. Your bowl should be loaded and brightly colored and steaming. Yum. To eat, stir everything around until it's well mixed and then dig in.

RAINBOW SALAD

DIFFICULTY: Medium • **MAKES:** 4 healthy servings

The best part about this side dish is that it's incredibly healthy. It's just loaded with vegetables. The worst part is that you can slice your fingers clean off while making it. At least, that's what I always think when I haul out the mandoline. It makes short work of the ingredients, yes, but it scares me so much that I have yet to let the kid use it. Chop saw, chainsaw, blowtorch: Yes. Mandoline: No. We all have boundaries—what can I say? If you have a mandoline, I advise taking the lead on cutting while the kiddo washes and mixes the ingredients. If you don't have a mandoline, let the kiddo slice away with a kitchen knife as you both create a salad that is bright and healthy and ridiculously yum.

Here's what you need:

TOOLS

❏ Mandoline with julienne blade, cutting board, mixing bowl

INGREDIENTS

❏ 2 carrots

❏ ½ small cabbage

❏ ½ jicama

❏ 1 apple

❏ Olive oil

❏ Salt and pepper to taste

❏ Mint or basil

Here's what you do:

1. First, have your kitchen helper wash the vegetables while you break out the mandoline.

2. Being careful to use the mandoline guard, run each vegetable and fruit over the slicer until you have perfectly sliced sticks of each kind. (I'm sure professional chefs reach a point when a mandoline doesn't give them the jeebies, but I'm not there yet. This is a great time to discuss tools and safety and how tools do great jobs of making short work of prep time but safety is always the first concern.)

3. When you're done julienning or slicing all the ingredients, add them to your mixing bowl and have your sous chef drizzle with a splash of oil and then sprinkle some salt and pepper and chopped mint or basil over everything. Let him use his clean hands to mix everything together. It's fun and slimy and a great way to mix everything up perfectly. Serve as a side to your favorite dinner.

BALSAMIC STEAK BITES

DIFFICULTY: Medium • **MAKES:** 12 bites

I've said it before and I'll say it again: Kids will eat just about anything on a toothpick. Add any type of dip and you're golden. This recipe features both. You're basically just cooking a steak here and turning it into hors d'oeuvres. But I like it because it's a great way to sneak in a steak night—I love meat—and provides a perfect game-night alternative to boring hot dogs or hamburgers.

Here's what you need:

TOOLS

❑ Stove, grill pan or frying pan, tongs, knife, cutting board, toothpicks, dipping cups or small bowls.

INGREDIENTS

❑ 1 large steak, about 8–10 ounces

❑ 1 teaspoon olive oil

❑ Salt and pepper

❑ 2 tablespoons balsamic vinegar (most syrupy you can find)

Here's what you do:

1 Coat steak in oil and salt and pepper and place in pan. I like to use a grill pan to mimic outdoor cooking, but a frying pan will do as well. Then cook it over medium heat, turning after about 7 minutes per side.

2 Once cooked and the steak has rested on a cutting board for a few minutes, cut into cubes. A good-sized steak will yield 12 or so. Slice off any fat or gristle, if the kiddos aren't fans. Then add toothpicks to each one and serve with a side of balsamic vinegar for dipping.

FIGGY PIGGY POUCHES

DIFFICULTY: Medium • **MAKES:** 1 pork chop

On the surface, this recipe almost sounds intimidating. Cooking meat in a sealed envelope of parchment paper, alongside a delightful combination of figs and garlic. In reality, it's as easy as tossing everything onto a piece of paper, folding it up, tossing it in the oven, and going on about your business. You don't really need to measure anything. You seriously just dump stuff together. This is an easy segue into new cooking techniques for kids.

Here's what you need:

TOOLS

❑ Oven, oven mitts, parchment paper, cookie sheet

INGREDIENTS

❑ 2 tablespoons olive oil

❑ 1 thick pork chop, about 6 ounces

❑ Salt and pepper to taste

❑ 5 ripe figs

❑ 5 garlic cloves

Here's what you do:

1 Preheat the oven to 400°F.

2 Unroll a piece of parchment paper that is about the size of your cookie sheet.

3 Now, splash some oil on the paper about 6" or 8" left or right of center. Put pork chop on oil. Salt and pepper the chop. Stack figs and peeled garlic cloves on and around the pork chop. Drizzle a bit of oil on everything again and sprinkle on some more salt and pepper.

4 Now, fold. Just fold the paper up until the ends meet, and then start to roll them together all around, forming a seal. Your pouch doesn't have to be perfect. Just make sure all ends are sealed. You basically want the pork and filling to steam in the pouch, so do your best to make it tight. You can always fold everything and then flip the package over onto the fold to make sure the edges don't unroll.

5 Pop it into the oven and cook for about 20–25 minutes, or until pork is done and the garlic is soft. Unroll pouch on serving plate to capture all the juices. Serve with rice or potatoes.

SUPER SLIDERS

DIFFICULTY: Medium • **MAKES:** 12 sliders

The great thing about this easy, fun take on traditional hamburgers is that you can customize them any way you like and make a whole batch of different flavor combinations to suit every family member's taste buds. While the meat is cooking, have your sous chef put out a "slider bar" of ingredients. This is a sure-fire movie night hit.

Here's what you need:

TOOLS

❑ Stove, grill pan, large mixing bowl, spatula, knife, cutting board, serving bowls, spoons

INGREDIENTS

❑ Cooking spray

❑ 1 pound ground beef (or chicken or turkey or—mmm—pork!)

❑ Salt and pepper dashes

❑ 1 tomato

❑ 6 slices cheese

❑ 1 package dinner rolls or slider buns

Here's what you do:

1 Spray grill pan with cooking spray and then turn burner to low-medium heat. Mix ground beef in mixing bowl with dashes of salt and pepper. Now, scoop out a small handful and form into a tiny patty—about half the size of a regular hamburger.

2 Cook sliders about 6 to 8 at a time. Flip after about 5 minutes and cook for an additional 5 minutes.

3 Now, here's where things get exciting. Add whatever you like. Grill an onion. Grill mushrooms. Use blue cheese, or triple cream cheese. Let your kids call the shots.

4 When the burgers are ready, put them on sliced dinner rolls, 2 to a plate. Let the kids go bonkers on toppings. Having a little control, I've found, motivates kids to eat what they create.

DAD TIP

If you can't find dinner rolls or slider buns, get regular hamburger buns and then use a drinking glass like a cookie cutter to cut out the perfect slider-sized bun. King Hawaiian brand rolls are also especially delicious and just the right size.

VEGGIE ROLLS

DIFFICULTY: Medium • **MAKES:** 4 rolls

This is straight from our favorite neighborhood Vietnamese takeout joint. But having take-out every night is expensive and not always good for you. So we made this veggie-heavy take on one of our favorites. It's fun to make, tastes great, and is crammed with healthy vegetables.

Here's what you need:

TOOLS

❑ Knife, cutting board, little serving bowls, big mixing bowl or pie pan, serving plate

INGREDIENTS

❑ 1 carrot

❑ 1 cucumber

❑ 1 red bell pepper

❑ ½ red cabbage

❑ 1 package rice paper rolls

❑ 2 cups water

❑ 4 tablespoons hoisin sauce

❑ Rice noodles, shrimp, cooked pork (all optional)

Here's what you do:

1 First get all your veggies ready, chopping everything into 4"-long, skinny strips. These are going to be your filling. Imagine them rolled up into paper. (I only use veggies for these, as rolls are fun to eat and great vehicles for greens consumption. But by all means, cook some rice noodles or rice and use that as a filling as well. This could easily become a full meal roll.)

2 When your veggies are ready to go, put them in serving bowls so the kids can choose how they want to make their own rolls.

3 Now, it's time to soak the rice paper rolls. They should come out of the package hard and brittle. Fill up your mixing bowl or pie pan with water and soak 1 or 2 papers at a time for about a minute. They should start to soften right away.

4 When they're super soft, gently remove from water, let water drip away, and put on cutting board or serving plate. Fill with as many delicious veggies as you want along one side. Roll that side up and tuck in the end flaps just before you finish the rolling. No worries if the ends are open. It may be messy but it'll be fun. Dip into hoisin sauce or your favorite dip and you're good to go.

LASAGNA CUP CAKES

DIFFICULTY: Hard • **MAKES:** 8 "cakes"

My Noni is probably having fits right now, as I'm calling lasagna *cake* and teaching you how to make individual ones instead of great big steaming platters fit for Sunday family dinners. If there's any consolation, these are still amazingly tasty and they're still great for a family dinner. You're basically going to make mini lasagnas in baking ramekins. You can individualize them any way you'd like. But I'm going to go with what my Noni would have liked—classic meat sauce with gooey cheese. As a cheat to make these easier for your sous chefs, I'm using store-bought Bolognese meat sauce, rather than making my own. You're already doing lots of little things to make the big picture, and premade sauce cuts down on time and mess.

Here's what you need:

TOOLS

❏ Oven, stove, microwave, cookie sheet, large pot, oven mitts, strainer, 8 (4") ramekins, spoons, knife, cutting board

INGREDIENTS

❏ 8 cups water

❏ 2 tablespoons salt

❏ 1 package lasagna noodles

❏ 1 can premade meat sauce (You can usually find good ones in the fresh pasta cooler area in 8-ounce tubs, rather than off-the-shelf cans. But even some of those are good. Usually 8–12 ounces is enough.)

❏ 1 cup ricotta cheese

❏ 1 cup shredded mozzarella cheese

❏ Sausage or mushrooms, if you don't use meat sauce (optional)

Here's what you do:

1 First things first: Preheat the oven to 375°F and bring a big pot of salted water to boil.

2 Cook your lasagna noodles when water comes to a boil—usually 10–11 minutes, but follow the instructions on the package you use. Drain water in strainer when cooked.

3 Heat sauce in microwave until just warm-ish or even slightly hot. You're going to cook in the oven soon enough, but this sort of starts it all off.

4 OK, now the fun begins. You'll repeat these next steps for each ramekin. First, add small spoonful of sauce to ramekin. Next, chop lasagna noodles to fit ramekin and add layer on bottom. Then add spoonful of ricotta and spread to cover pasta. Spoon in meat sauce and sprinkle with some mozzarella. Now add one more layer of pasta, and then ricotta, and then meat sauce and mozzarella. Repeat until you have one last layer of meat sauce. Sprinkle with mozzarella cheese.

5 When all your ramekins are ready, put on cookie sheet and pop into oven. Cook for about a half hour to melt everything into a gooey, meaty, cheese-y, delicious personalized lasagna cake. When you serve, be sure to warn the kiddos that the ramekin is hot. They'll learn after a few touches. Enjoy.

STUFFED RED PEPPERS

DIFFICULTY: Medium • **MAKES:** 4 stuffed peppers

Right under "food on sticks" on kids' list of Things That Are Fun to Eat is "things that are stuffed." These peppers won't disappoint. They're cool to make since you get to shove in all that yummy filling—then there's a whole second round of fun when you eat the filling out of the pepper. Plus, as the chief dishwasher, I'm always a fan of eating out of food vessels because it usually means less cleaning. With stuffed red peppers, you have a great carb (rice) cooked inside a fantastic vegetable (pepper). Serve as a complement to salmon fillets or chicken or steak and you have a wonderful meal that is also healthy. And doesn't require a boatload of dishes.

Here's what you need:

TOOLS

❏ Oven, microwave, cookie sheet, oven mitts, mixing bowl, cheese grater, measuring cups and spoons, knife, cutting board

INGREDIENTS

❏ 1 packet 90-second instant rice

❏ ½ cup grated mozzarella (or other) cheese

❏ ¼ cup frozen peas

❏ 2 tablespoons olive oil

❏ Salt and pepper dashes

❏ 4 medium-sized red bell peppers

Here's what you do:

1 Preheat the oven to 375°F.

2 Heat up the packet of rice. I love these silly things. It's a total cheat and I don't even care.

3 When the rice is done, dump into a mixing bowl and add the cheese. You can grate any kind you like. Now add the peas and 1 tablespoon of olive oil along with a few dashes of salt and pepper. Your filling is ready.

4 Now it's time to move on to the peppers. Slice off the tops like you would slice off a pumpkin top for carving, but don't discard them. Now scoop out all the innards and wash everything down. You're good to go.

5 Fill the peppers with your rice, cheese, and pea mix and then put the tops back on like jaunty little hats. They don't have to fit on perfectly.

6 I always like this part. Drizzle a little oil on each pepper and use your hands to run it all over the hat and the sides. This is perfect for super small sous chefs. The sous sous chefs, if you will.

7 Now put the peppers on a cookie sheet and bake for about 30 minutes. The filling should be nice and hot and the outside of the pepper should be cooked but not falling apart with softness.

MAC AND CHEESY

DIFFICULTY: Medium-hard • **MAKES:** 4 servings

I gotta admit: The pull of store-bought boxed macaroni and cheese is like some Death Star begging ray put on repeat: "Can we? Can we? Can we?" We buy them from time to time . . . but man, the sodium content always gets me. There's usually just a ton of it. It's a nice once-in-a-while treat, sure, but not as fun as making your own gooey batches of nature's miracle comfort food. Have your sous chef give this a spin and compare to his favorite boxed brand. I'd wager this wins.

Here's what you need:

TOOLS

❑ Oven, stove, large pot, large saucepan, 9" × 13" baking or casserole dish, oven mitts, cheese grater, measuring cups and spoons, stirring spoons, strainer

INGREDIENTS

❑ 1 cup uncooked elbow macaroni (the cool thing about DIY is that you can choose any short, cut pasta you want)

❑ 2 tablespoons butter

❑ 2 tablespoons all-purpose flour

❑ Salt and pepper pinches

❑ ¼ teaspoon dry mustard

❑ 1 cup milk

❑ 1½ cups grated Cheddar cheese

❑ 2 tablespoons breadcrumbs

Here's what you do:

1 Preheat the oven to 350°F and bring a large pot of water to boil.

2 Cook macaroni in water until done—usually 10 or so minutes—while you grate the cheese and measure out other ingredients.

3 In a large saucepan, melt butter over medium heat and then reduce to low heat.

4 Now add flour, salt, pepper, and mustard. Stir until smooth.

5 Add milk and cheese and keep stirring until the cheese melts and the sauce is creamy, smooth, and looks like, well, macaroni and cheese sauce.

6 Drain pasta when it's done and add to your cheese sauce. Stir it around until well mixed and then spread out in your baking or casserole dish.

7 Sprinkle breadcrumbs all over the mac and cheese. This will provide a nice crunch.

8 Now cook for about 30–40 minutes until heated all the way through and the top is golden brown. Let cool a few minutes before serving.

DAD TIP

You can also pour the mac and cheese mix into a pie pan, bake in that, and then let cool completely after baking. Give it a slice and all of a sudden you have mac and cheese pie. How cool is that?

ROLL YOUR OWN SUSHI

DIFFICULTY: Medium • **MAKES:** 6 rolls

My daughter is a sushi nut. For her birthday, she wanted to visit her favorite restaurant for oma-kase, which basically translates to "I leave it to you." You put yourself in the sushi chef's hands and eat whatever is presented to you. Good call, kid, good call. That was a birthday meal memorable to everyone. Baby tuna. Octopus. Grilled eel. Horse mackerel. Uni. Oysters. You name it, we ate it. Everything tasted of the sea and of just-barely-sweet rice. While it would be difficult for us to find such perfect ingredients for at-home dinners—not to mention ridiculously expensive—we've found we can replicate the fun times with a few kitchen staples and a DIY sensibility.

Here's what you need:

TOOLS

- ❏ Knife, cutting board, cling wrap, lots of serving bowls, sushi-making bamboo mat if you have one—no biggie if not

INGREDIENTS

- ❏ 1 cup sushi rice
- ❏ 1 salmon fillet
- ❏ 1 carrot
- ❏ 1 cucumber
- ❏ 1 avocado
- ❏ 6 sheets of nori (maybe some extras just in case)
- ❏ 1 cup water in a bowl you can easily get your hands in
- ❏ 1 wasabi can or squeeze tube
- ❏ ¼ cup soy sauce

Here's what you do:

1 First things first: Cook your rice. The package should tell you how. If you want, at the end you can sweeten it up like a sushi chef would with a splash of rice vinegar and maybe a sprinkle of sugar, but you don't need to. When done cooking, let cool in a bowl for a tiny bit. Should be just barely warm.

2 While the rice is cooking and cooling, prepare your fish. I like to use a nice salmon fillet grilled over medium-low heat for about 7 minutes per side. I like it just pinkish-orange in the middle.

3 So now you've got your rice cooking and cooling and your salmon cooking. Have your sous chef prepare all the vegetables by slicing each into long, thin strips. Save the avocado for last.

4 When all your ingredients are ready, you're ready to roll. Literally. Unwrap a square of cling wrap and lay flat on cutting board. Now rest nori on it. Being sure to dip your fingers in water first—it keeps the rice from sticking to your fingers—grab a ball of rice and spread it out on ¾ of 1 sheet of the nori. Just pat it down and smooth it as best as you can. It doesn't have to be super thick—just enough to cover up the green of the nori. Dip your fingers into water when it gets sticky.

5 Now, here's the cool part. Emme likes salmon and avocado alone. I like a little crunch, so I add carrots and cukes. Lay down a thin line of veggies—1 or 2 strips per veggie—in the middle of the rice. Make a similar line of salmon right on top of veggies.

6 Now, roll! Pretend the first one is a practice one. That always helps me get in the right mindset. Dip hands in water and then just roll the side with rice on it, rolling away from you toward the end without rice on it. The rice-loaded nori may feel fat and hard to roll and that's fine. Sometimes the nori tears. That's cool, too. It happens. Cut your sous chef some slack if this is her first time making sushi. Maybe take out some veggies or salmon next time. You don't have to roll super tight, just enough to turn it into a roll about the width of a D battery.

7 So now you have a rollish-looking thing. Use your fingers to wet the edge of the nori that doesn't have rice on it and then stick it down on the roll you just made. You can roll your roll with cling wrap and press it a little tighter if you like. The cling wrap keeps everything together, as you press or even roll it with the palms of your hands on the board. Again, it doesn't have to be super tight—just firm enough to be roll-like. If you have a sushi mat, place over top and press down on top and sides. If you don't, no worries. Cling wrap alone works fine.

8 When it feels roll-y, congrats. You're done! Keep the cling wrap on and use a super sharp knife to cut the roll into circles. Serve with a side of mixed wasabi-soy sauce to taste.

DAD TIP

If the rolling is driving you crazy, make easier "hand rolls" instead. Simply take the nori and roll it into a cone. Dump in your rice and then add salmon and veggies. Enjoy!

SWEETEST POTATO, BACON, AND EGG HASH

DIFFICULTY: Hard • **MAKES:** 2–3 servings

This recipe is . . . involved. In one pan, you'll have a hash going and a lot of moving parts. In another pan, you'll have a simple fried egg cooking at the last minute. Add in the difficulty of preparing raw sweet potato and this is a recipe for an older kid to tackle with a little help. But oh man, the payoff is worth it. Drizzle with maple syrup and you've got a breakfast-for-dinner family hit for the ages.

Here's what you need:

TOOLS

❏ Stove, 1 large frying pan with lid, 1 small or medium pan with lid, veggie peeler, knife, cutting board, measuring cups and spoons, spatula

INGREDIENTS

❏ 1 large sweet potato, or 2 narrow ones

❏ ¼ cup chopped red onion

❏ ¼ cup chopped red bell pepper

❏ 3 strips bacon

❏ 1 tablespoon butter

❏ 2 tablespoons olive oil, divided

❏ 1 tablespoon water

❏ 2–3 eggs, depending on how many people serving

❏ Salt and pepper to taste

❏ Finely chopped jalapeño adds a little nice heat for kids who like it. Sriracha sauce does the same at the end as well. Syrup makes for a fun taste treat as well. (All optional.)

Here's what you do:

1 Dice your sweet potato into cubes about ¾" to 1" big. That's the end product. To get there, first peel off skin with peeler. Then either cut disks and chop those down or cut the whole thing in half lengthwise and lay flat side down on cutting board for more stability when dicing. To be honest, I'm not a huge fan of this whole process, as sweet potatoes are hard for me to cut. Get the long, narrow ones to make it easier.

2 While you're at it, chop up your bacon. You're going for bite-sized here. Then set aside all ingredients and get ready to cook.

3 Melt 1 tablespoon butter in large frying pan over medium-high heat. Add chopped bacon. Let it start to sizzle.

4 Next, add sweet potatoes in a single layer, or as close as you can get. Add a drizzle of oil and a splash of water—about 1 tablespoon each. Top with lid and cook for about 5 minutes. This steams the sweet potato and cooks the inside. It doesn't do wonders for the bacon but we'll fix that.

5 Now, remove lid and inch heat up to high. Cook for another 5 minutes without stirring. Let the bottom char.

6 As that's going, work on a Simple Fried Egg recipe (see recipe in Chapter 2). Yes, you can always wait until done with the hash before moving on to the eggs. But this is a great time for teamwork, or even to let your more experienced chef start working on the timing of plating a finished, more complicated meal.

7 Now that the bottom of your hash is charred, do your best to flip pieces and chunks over to turn the hash without mushing or breaking the pieces. Just gently insert spatula underneath, lift, and turn.

8 Add onions and peppers—and a pinch of salt and pepper, and perhaps a drizzle of more oil if too charry—and then flip everything around again.

9 Cook for an additional 5 minutes and plate. The sweet potato should be charred and fried on the outside but soft on the inside. The bacon should be crispy and the onions and peppers in that middle space between done and slightly crunchy.

10 Now plate the hash and top with your fried eggs. You can also add an Arzak egg to this for a super special treat, but save that one for amazing, experienced chefs.

11 Eat as is or drizzle with hot sauce and syrup. Oh man, you're in for a treat.

BANANA LEAF SALMON

DIFFICULTY: Medium • **MAKES:** 1 serving

The first time I made this, it took me half a day to find the banana leaves. I drove around town to every single grocery store and eventually headed to a nearby big city. No luck. Little did I know that our local Asian superstore had just what I was looking for. Long story short: You can probably find the banana leaves at your local Asian superstore, or, perhaps, online. It's worth the hunt, however, as these salmon fillets made in little banana leaf pouches are incredibly fun to make and also so delicious.

Here's what you need:

TOOLS
❏ Oven, cookie sheet, oven mitts, knife, cutting board

INGREDIENTS
❏ 1 banana leaf

❏ 1 (4-ounce) salmon fillet

❏ 1 tablespoon olive oil

❏ Salt and pepper

❏ 1 lemon

❏ 1 sprig basil

Here's what you do:

1 Preheat the oven to 400°F.

2 Unroll a whole banana leaf, rinse it, and place on your cutting board. Then place the salmon in the middle of it.

3 Drizzle the salmon with olive oil and salt and pepper. Cut half a lemon into thin circles and lay those circles on top of the salmon. Squeeze a little juice from other half of lemon onto fillet.

4 Now you're ready to roll. Try to keep the salmon and all those juices where they are and fold the sides of the banana leaf over the salmon and then fold the end lengths together. You can at this point flip over the whole package so that the seams are face down. Put the whole packet on an ungreased cookie sheet.

5 Bake the packet for 8 minutes and remove. Let cool for about 3 minutes and then just flop the whole packet onto your plate. Let the kiddos open the special treat. Don't eat the leaf; instead, maybe serve with rice or couscous—anything that will soak up the juices that pour out.

EASY RICOTTA GNOCCHI WITH BROWNED BUTTER, HERBS, AND CHEESE

Contributed by Chris Routly

DIFFICULTY: Medium-hard • **MAKES:** 6–8 servings

My friend Chris Routly is a man of many, many wonderful hats. He's a stay-at-home dad in Portland, Oregon, to two amazing boys, Tucker and Coltrane. He's also an incredible writer behind the website *www.Daddydoctrines.com*, and several graphic novels and children's books. (My daughter read his *Life of Ronnie* comic book three times. In a row. And I think his latest children's book, *Sometimes You Need a Jellyfish*, is going to be a huge hit, just you watch.) As if that's not talent enough, Chris is a whiz in the kitchen and creator of one of my all-time favorite breakfast treats: The Puffin. It's a pancake/muffin amalgamation that is sure to please anyone (check out his cool website for even more). I was so impressed that I asked him to contribute a favorite family meal, and Chris does not disappoint. You're going to appreciate not only the taste but the detailed preparation of these gnocchi. It's a process that makes the kitchen feel like a warm, family fun-time event. Take it away, Chris:

I love cooking with my kids. Not only is it fun; it helps encourage them to get excited about trying new foods and it also teaches them a life skill that they will use for the rest of their lives. Many of my fondest childhood memories involve being able to help my parents or grandmother make some tasty treats. I love passing that on to my boys.

A few of the great things about making ricotta gnocchi: it is very easy, it involves rolling out dough into awesome snakes, it is very forgiving as far as shaping the actual gnocchi themselves goes, and it is super adaptable to your family's tastes. This is a perfect dinner for letting your kids take the lead on cooking, with you there to help guide them as needed.

Here's what you need:

TOOLS

❏ Stove, large pot, large frying pan, baking rack or parchment-lined baking sheet, oven mitts, measuring cups and spoons, large mixing bowl, dough cutter or knife, large cutting board, fork, large slotted spoon, large bowl for ice bath

INGREDIENTS

❏ 2 cups whole-milk ricotta

❏ 2 large eggs, lightly beaten

❏ 1½ cups grated Parmigiano-Reggiano cheese, divided

❏ ¼ teaspoon freshly grated nutmeg

❏ 3 tablespoons plus ¼ teaspoon salt, divided

❏ ¼ teaspoon freshly ground pepper

❏ 1¼ cups all-purpose flour

❏ Ice

❏ ½ stick unsalted butter

❏ Fresh herbs (such as rosemary, sage, oregano, and basil)

❏ Salt and pepper to taste

Here's what you do:

1 Fill a pot with water and bring to a boil.

2 In a large bowl, stir together ricotta, eggs, 1 cup of the Parmigiano-Reggiano, nutmeg, and ¼ teaspoon each of salt and pepper.

3 Add the flour and stir to form a wet dough.

4 On a well-floured cutting board, table, or countertop, dump out dough and shape into several 1" thick snakes with your hands (flouring your hands makes this much easier).

5 With a dough cutter or knife, cut each snake across, into 1" pieces. This recipe will make approximately 48 1" pieces, but if you'd prefer, simply cut them smaller and make more.

6 (Optional, but suggested!) Roll each piece on a gnocchi board, the back of a fork, or along a wire baking rack, in order to make small ridges. These will help hold the sauce later, and give the gnocchi a nice rustic texture. As you go, lay each piece onto the baking rack or parchment-lined baking sheet.

7 At this point the pieces can be refrigerated or frozen, if you are making them ahead of time.

8 When the water is at a rolling boil, salt the water (about 3 tablespoons for 6 quarts of water) and then begin adding the gnocchi a few at a time. You will want to prepare them in at least 2 batches.

9 Cook gnocchi for 3–4 minutes per batch, until they float and are cooked through (you can remove one and cut it open to check if dough is cooked fully). While they cook, prepare an ice bath—just cubes in a clean, large bowl.

10 Remove gnocchi with a slotted spoon, drain, and then add to the ice bath for a few minutes to stop cooking and cool, before transferring back to the baking sheet.

11 Repeat with next batch, until all gnocchi is cooked.

12 When you are almost ready to eat, bring a large frying pan to medium-low heat and cook butter and fresh herbs until butter is golden brown (about 5 minutes).

13 Add gnocchi to frying pan, sprinkle with remaining ½ cup cheese, and toss. Allow gnocchi to heat up and brown slightly. Season with salt and pepper to taste.

14 Serve hot, with more cheese, to your grateful family and friends!

DAD TIP
from the Routly Kitchen

This basic recipe works well for experimenting with different variations. Like mushrooms? Add some to the dough and the sauce! Have a lot of basil on hand? Chop some up and add it to the dough, and serve the gnocchi with your favorite pesto! The sky's the limit!

BOTTOM-OF-THE-BUCKET DRUMSTICKS

DIFFICULTY: Medium • **MAKES:** 8 chicken drumsticks

Sometimes being the youngest child in a houseful of brothers meant I got the short end of the stick. Literally. Whenever my mom would bring home a bucket of that famous fast-food fried chicken, I'd start to water at the mouth, eager to dig through the bucket for a cherished drumstick. Everyone's favorite. Of course, if I didn't get there first, my brothers would raid the bucket like locusts. With this recipe, I tried to put a healthier spin on a traditional fast-food favorite and make it something kids can do solo. Plus, they get all the drumsticks they want . . .

Here's what you need:

TOOLS
❑ Oven, baking pan, oven mitts, measuring cups and spoons, 2 pie plates or big shallow bowls, spoon, 2 sets of tongs

INGREDIENTS
❑ 1 cup milk

❑ 3 tablespoons flour

❑ 1 cup corn flakes

❑ ½ teaspoon paprika

❑ 1 teaspoon salt

❑ 1 teaspoon pepper

❑ 8 chicken legs

Here's what you do:

1 Preheat the oven to 375°F.

2 First, you're going to make an assembly line to coat the chicken. Please keep everything clean and be careful where you touch and store raw chicken, as a salmonella outbreak is never good for anyone. When you're done, wash your hands, the dishes, and the workspace thoroughly.

3 To start, pour the milk into one of the pie plates.

4 Next, put flour, corn flakes, and all your spices into the other pie plate. Use your fists or a spoon to really crunch up all the corn flakes. I like small bits, not big flakes.

5 When everything is ready to go, use one set of tongs to roll a drumstick in the milk, and then drop it gently into the corn flake mix. Use another set of tongs just for the corn flake mix to roll the drumstick around. Remove with those tongs and then place on baking pan. Repeat with all your drumsticks until done. (I like to have one place on a cutting board to set one pair of tongs and then another place on the same cutting board to place other tongs. Then it's easy to see where you rested anything that touched chicken and makes it all easier to clean.)

6 Bake for 35 to 45 minutes until drumsticks are fully cooked and coating is toasty brown. Enjoy!

EASY TACO TUESDAY

DIFFICULTY: Medium • **MAKES:** 6–8 tacos

A small tortilla is the perfect vehicle for consuming pretty much anything. You can throw meat and cheese on one and have a traditional taco, or dice up some tofu and toss in some hummus and kale and all of a sudden you have a unique pre-practice or after-school fill-up. We keep a stash of small corn tortillas in the pantry as a quick and easy DIY meal—just like this Easy Taco Tuesday. You can customize it any way your sous chef wants.

Here's what you need:

TOOLS

❑ Stove, large frying pan, knife, cutting board, cheese grater, measuring cups and spoons, stirring spoon, small serving bowls

INGREDIENTS

❑ 1 pound ground turkey

❑ 1 white onion

❑ 1 tomato

❑ Lettuce to make ¼ cup shredded

❑ Cheddar or queso fresco cheese, to grate into ¼ cup

❑ Few sprigs cilantro

❑ 1 avocado

❑ 1 teaspoon taco seasoning, or just salt and pepper if you want

❑ 1 tablespoon water

❑ 2 tortillas

Here's what you do:

1 In a large frying pan, brown the ground turkey over medium heat. Drain excess fat when done.

2 While meat is cooking, dice the white onion into small bits. Chop the tomato as well and shred the lettuce. Just wash it and chop it into thin strips. Now grate the cheese and chop the cilantro, removing the stems.

3 When the meat is done and your veggies prepped, add taco seasoning to meat and 1 tablespoon water before stirring and cooking for an additional 2–3 minutes. Then dump it into one of your serving bowls.

4 I like to heat up the tortillas a tiny bit in the frying pan. This makes them easier to fold and a little tastier. When your tortillas are warm, you're ready to serve. Slice your avocado in half and spoon out some slices, if you like. Let your sous chef fill her own and go to town on an easy-peasy meal that is sure to please.

DAD TIP

Tacos (and burritos) are absolutely perfect for any leftovers from last night's dinner. I like to shred rotisserie chicken and simply heat it up in the microwave before adding to a tortilla with avocado and a few tablespoons of salsa. But let your sous chefs experiment with their own fillings. Pretty soon they'll be making their own meals.

SWEET GINGER CARROT SOUP

DIFFICULTY: Medium • **MAKES:** 4–6 servings

I'm a big fan of carrots. And this is an amazing soup to showcase their sweet deliciousness. But what I like best about it is that you can easily substitute different veggies. You can use butternut squash instead, or even green beans. The cooking process is generally the same—steam and char your veggies in a big pan, and then mash them up and add stock and cream. The soup is warm, creamy, homey, and just right for a cold night.

Here's what you need:

TOOLS

❑ Stove, frying pan with lid, measuring cups, immersion blender (or regular blender or food processor)

INGREDIENTS

❑ 1 batch of Sweet Ginger Carrots (see recipe in Chapter 6)

❑ 3 cups chicken stock, divided

❑ ¼ cup heavy cream

Here's what you do:

1 First things first: Make your Sweet Ginger Carrots. Instead of serving them when finished, however, you're going to do a little magic in the very same pan.

2 When the carrots are done, add about 1 cup of your chicken stock and then use an immersion blender to blend everything together. If you don't have an immersion blender, transfer the ingredients to a full-sized blender or food processor. Give everything a whole bunch of whirs until it's smooth, and then transfer back to your pan.

3 Turn the heat to medium-high and add the rest of your stock and your heavy cream. When it's hot and begins to bubble, turn to low again. You're basically done at this point. Seriously, it's that easy. Make veggies, add stock and cream, and then boom! Soup. It's on.

DAD TIP

As a unique topping, I like to fry up a few strips of bacon until they're nice and crispy and then crumble them over the carrot soup.

Sides have always been an afterthought for me, to be honest. The first meal I ever cooked for my soon-to-be wife (thank God she stayed) consisted of a perfectly cooked flanked steak arranged beautifully on a cutting board with rosemary sprigs as decoration.

"That's nice," she said, "But where are the . . . sides?"

Thankfully, I've discovered just how important sides are and how they can add complexity to meals or complement the perfect main course—not to mention the fact that sides are usually veggies, and kids (and adults) need lots of them. From delightful kale potatoes to a corn and mint and cheese salad that will delight your taste buds, you'll find sides for every occasion.

FRIED RICE CAKES

DIFFICULTY: Hard • **MAKES:** 12 cakes

My wife is an expert at making these little guys. They're crispy and hot and delicious. You can serve them on their own, or topped with an egg for a magical meal, or as a side to a lighter protein, such as fish. They are, however, heavy and fried, so I like to serve them with a nice salad or veggies on the side.

Here's what you need:

TOOLS

❑ Stove, large frying pan, measuring cups and spoons, 2 mixing bowls, whisk, circular metal cookie cutter, spatula

INGREDIENTS

❑ 2 cups cooked white rice

❑ 1 tablespoon flour

❑ 1 teaspoon sesame oil

❑ ¼ cup cooked edamame

❑ Salt and pepper to taste

❑ 1 egg

❑ 2 tablespoons vegetable oil

❑ Cooking spray

❑ Hot sauce to taste

Here's what you do:

1 Dump the rice into a mixing bowl. Add flour, sesame oil, edamame, and salt and pepper.

2 In a separate bowl, whisk the egg and then add to rice mixture. Mix everything around until it's nice and coated. The egg and flour will bind the rice together while cooking. If it doesn't quite feel sticky enough, add a touch more flour and maybe a splash of water. It should be sort of tacky.

3 Now, the hard part. Heat up your frying pan to medium and then add 1 tablespoon vegetable oil and let it heat not quite to smoking.

4 Spray the inside of your cookie cutter with cooking spray. Now put cutter in pan and spoon in some rice mixture and pat down until they're the size of, say, a coffee mug bottom. Jiggle the cutter a little with a cooking tool and then remove gently. (You really don't have to use a cookie cutter. You could just spoon in a bit of rice mixture and then use your spatula to flatten it.)

5 Cook for about 3 or 4 minutes per side, or until each side is crispy and brown. The thicker you make them, the creamier they are inside while the outside remains crispy.

SWEET POTATO FRIES

DIFFICULTY: Medium • **MAKES:** 4 servings

I love these simple fries because they're thick and meaty. They form a perfect char and create a hearty side dish to hamburgers or steak. Plus, sweet potatoes are just so good for you.

Here's what you need:

TOOLS

❑ Oven, cookie sheet, oven mitts, potato peeler, knife, cutting board, mandoline, large mixing bowl

INGREDIENTS

❑ 2 medium to large sweet potatoes

❑ 1 tablespoon olive oil

❑ Salt and pepper to taste

Here's what you do:

1 Preheat the oven to 400°F.

2 Wash your potatoes. This is a perfect task for the little chef in the house.

3 Slice your potatoes in half lengthwise and then cut those lengths in half widthwise so that you end up with 4 pieces per potato.

4 Now you're ready for the mandoline. Slap on the medium-sized blades. These create those thicker fries you've probably seen in restaurants. They are yummy.

5 Being careful to use the guard and not slice off your fingers, cut the potatoes until you have lots of uncooked fries. If you don't have a mandoline, just use a knife.

6 This is a fun part for the kids. Toss the fries into a large mixing bowl, drizzle with oil, sprinkle with salt and pepper, and then have the kids stick their clean hands in and mix everything around.

7 Once the fries are well mixed, spread them onto a cookie sheet in a single layer. Cook for 10–12 minutes and then check doneness with knife. The knife should slide easily into a fry and the skins should be crispy. Give it a few more minutes if you're not there yet and check again.

8 Now, restaurants will take out the fries and sprinkle with salt again. I've got blood pressure that reads like an altimeter, so I skip this step. I realize that salty fries, however, are delicious, so feel free to flavor to your own taste and enjoy.

KALE MASHED POTATOES

Contributed by Jason and Lucy Sperber

DIFFICULTY: Medium • **MAKES:** 4–6 servings

My friend Jason Sperber is a stay-at-home dad to two amazing girls, Lucy and Emi. He is, like me, also an incurable foodie, and I am grateful for our time wandering Austin together as we searched for the perfect breakfast tacos. Jason writes the blog *Daddy in a Strange Land* (*http:// daddyinastrangeland.wordpress.com* and on Twitter *@dad_strangeland*) about his adventures on the home front. He also posts incredible recipes and food photos on social media, how we mainly stay in touch nowadays. I'm proud and happy to offer one of his family's favorite recipes as a perfect side dish or even a meal on its own. So without further ado, let me hand it over to Jason:

I've been cooking a variation on this dish for almost two decades, since discovering Deborah Madison's Vegetarian Cooking for Everyone. *Feel empowered to play with the recipe according to your family's tastes. I used to replace a third of the potatoes with other root vegetables like celeriac. In its current form, it has evolved to be a weekly staple in our home, with both girls requesting it alongside teriyaki salmon, pan-seared turkey cutlets, or grilled steak.*

Here's what you need:

TOOLS

❑ Stove, large pot, large pan, knife, cutting board, strainer, measuring spoons, potato masher or fork

INGREDIENTS

❑ 2 bunches Tuscan kale (a.k.a. black kale, lacinato kale, dinosaur kale, or cavolo nero)

❑ 2 pounds gold potatoes

❑ 2 garlic cloves

❑ 2 tablespoons extra virgin olive oil, plus more for drizzle

❑ Pinch red pepper flakes

❑ Salt and pepper to taste

❑ 2 tablespoons crème fraîche

Here's what you do:

1 Put a large pot of salted water on to boil.

2 Trim kale stems by folding leaves in half lengthwise and cutting hard stems out. Then stack leaves, roll tightly lengthwise, and slice thinly, also called shredding or making "chiffonade."

3 Rinse shredded kale and place in boiling water for 6 minutes. While kale is boiling, peel and quarter potatoes.

4 Remove boiled kale to a strainer, leaving the water boiling in the pot, and press as much liquid out of the kale as possible. Once the kale is out of the pot, add the potatoes to the boiling water and cook for 12 minutes or until soft.

5 As the potatoes cook, peel and slice garlic. Heat olive oil in a large pan over medium heat and add garlic and red pepper flakes.

6 When the garlic is fragrant, add drained kale, stirring to coat with oil. Add salt and pepper to taste and more oil if dry. Turn the heat down to low and cover, stirring occasionally, until the potatoes are done.

7 When potatoes are done, drain and add to pan with kale. Mash with a fork or potato masher to desired consistency. Season with salt and pepper to taste, adding oil if dry. Stir to combine evenly, and turn off heat.

8 Now add crème fraîche and stir to combine. Drizzle with extra virgin olive oil before serving.

DAD TIP
from the Sperber Kitchen

The crème fraîche can be replaced with butter if preferred, or dairy can be left out entirely for a vegan dish. Add a squeeze of fresh lemon juice at the end to brighten the dish.

QUIN . . . WHAT? SALAD

DIFFICULTY: Medium • **MAKES:** 4 servings

Quinoa seems like one of those crazy new fads that will flash across the dining scene and then disappear like so many carob chips. I admit that the first time I saw the word, I couldn't even come close to pronouncing it. Kw-eye-no-ah? Nope, it's KEEN-wah. But oh man, it's become a staple in our house. Bigtime. It's just loaded with protein and can take all manner of additions. It's pretty hard to ruin. I throw it in salad or serve it as a side. You can toast it and then cook it, steam it, bake it. I like to make big batches of this lemon quinoa salad to serve as a side or as a salad toss-in on busy nights.

Here's what you need:

TOOLS

❏ Stove, pot with lid, measuring cups and spoons, knife, cutting board, strainer, serving bowl, mixing spoon

INGREDIENTS

❏ 2 cups water

❏ 1 cup quinoa

❏ 1 small bunch cilantro

❏ ¼ cup minced red bell pepper

❏ ¼ cup minced red onion

❏ 2 tablespoons raisins

❏ 2 tablespoons pine nuts

❏ Salt and pepper

❏ 1 lemon

❏ 1 tablespoon olive oil

Here's what you do:

1 Let's get the quinoa started before moving on to all the stuff you're going to add to it. First, boil the water. When it's rolling, add the quinoa. Now reduce the heat to low and cover with lid. Cook for 12–14 minutes.

2 While the quinoa is simmering, get everything else ready. Chop the cilantro into a small mince. We like teeny tiny bits, so we chop it up well. Everything else can hang back until the quinoa is done.

3 When the quinoa is done, strain and dump into your serving bowl. Fluff it around a bit with the spoon to make sure it doesn't feel too steamy.

4 Now dump in the raisins, the nuts, the pepper, onion, and some salt and pepper. Slice the lemon in half and squeeze in a whole bunch of juice. Drizzle with olive oil and fluff around a bit more. Serve as a side or on its own. Store any leftovers in an airtight container for a couple of days.

BAKED POTATO BAR

DIFFICULTY: Medium • **MAKES:** 1 potato

This is a simple baked potato gone wild. What I love is that your little one can absolutely make this his own. He can fill up all the topping bowls and then add them to a potato in any way or amount he likes. There's something about the control and creativity of making this himself that will surely make him proud. These are great for parties or sleepovers too, because everyone gets a potato the way they like 'em. I love them on lazy fall days, because they take awhile to bake so you can hang out and play in the meantime.

Here's what you need:

TOOLS
- ❑ Oven, oven mitts, cookie sheet, knife, bowls (for as many toppings as you want)

INGREDIENTS
- ❑ 1 large potato
- ❑ 1 teaspoon olive oil
- ❑ Salt and pepper to taste
- ❑ 1 tablespoon butter
- ❑ ¼ cup grated cheese (any you like)
- ❑ 1 dollop sour cream
- ❑ 2 tablespoons salsa
- ❑ 1 teaspoon bacon bits
- ❑ (You get the idea. Use whatever toppings you like: broccoli florets, meat, edamame . . .)

Here's what you do:

1 Preheat oven to 350°F while you wash your potato and poke it a few times with a knife or a fork.

2 Smear potato with olive oil and then sprinkle with salt and pepper. Then place on cookie sheet and put in oven for about 45 to 55 minutes. Stick a knife in it to check if it's done. The knife should slide in easily.

3 While the potato is finishing its business in the oven, get to work on the toppings. If you're just making a fast meal at home, you can open up some containers and add a spoon to them, serving from the container. If you want to make a bigger deal of it (or your chef does), add toppings to bowls and arrange in the middle of the table with spoons for serving. It always reminds me of a fancy buffet bar and kids love it.

4 When the potato is done, have your sous chef slice it open end to end and carefully peel open with fork. It's going to be hot, so watch out.

5 Once the potato is open and plated, add anything you like. (I like to add butter first and then close back up for a minute, so it melts really well.)

DAD TIP

Keep the oven on while you're eating. When you get to the point where all the middle is gone and the skins remain, put the skins on a cookie sheet again, drizzle with oil, and top with more grated cheese. Put in oven for 5 or so minutes and you'll have crispy, cheesy skins that will be gone in a flash.

ROASTED CORN, MINT, AND CHEESE SALAD

DIFFICULTY: Medium • **MAKES:** 4 servings

You're thinking: Corn, mint, and . . . cheese? I know, I know, it sounds odd. But I had something similar in a Mexican restaurant in San Francisco and knew right away that the flavor combination was perfect for kids and that with a few tweaks here and there they could make it all on their own.

Here's what you need:

TOOLS

❑ Stove, large frying pan, knife, cutting board, wooden spoon or spatula

INGREDIENTS

❑ 2 ears of corn

❑ 1 tablespoon butter

❑ Salt and pepper, to taste

❑ 1 sprig of mint

❑ ¼ cup feta cheese

Here's what you do:

1 Have the kiddos husk the corn. It's a great lesson in food prep.

2 Heat the frying pan to medium and melt the butter while your sous chef slices the corn. Chop off the bottom so you have a stable base (you need some force to get through the ear, so you might have to do this part). Stand the corn up so the pointing end is vertical. Shear off the kernels, slicing from top to bottom.

3 Toss kernels into the frying pan. Cook for about 7 minutes or so, sprinkling with salt and pepper. (Not too much salt, as the cheese is pretty salty.) Stir only occasionally, as you want the kernels to develop a nice char in places. Be careful, sometimes the kernels pop and jump.

4 While the corn is cooking, chop the mint and crumble the feta.

5 When you're ready to take the corn off the burner, add the mint and feta and then stir. Remove, plate, and revel in the sweet, charry, cheesy deliciousness.

TOMATO PEACH MOZZARELLA SALAD

DIFFICULTY: Medium • **MAKES:** 2 servings

There's an old joke about avocados and their readiness for eating: Not yet, not yet, not yet, eat me, too late. This salad is a little like that, only with peaches and tomatoes. Find some that are just ready to eat that day—they should smell like, well, like ripe tomatoes and peaches—and I promise you'll have a salad you'll never forget. Maybe save this one for a day you take a family trip to a farmers' market and then return with table-ready produce. Because it involves some simple cutting and a little splashing of ingredients, it's perfect for young chefs learning knife skills.

Here's what you need:

TOOLS

❏ Knife, cutting board, large mixing bowl

INGREDIENTS

❏ 2 ripe tomatoes

❏ 1 ripe white or regular peach (nectarines work as well)

❏ ½ cup buffalo mozzarella cheese, or the wettest, best you can find

❏ 1 sprig basil

❏ 1 capful olive oil

❏ 2 capfuls white balsamic vinegar

❏ Salt and pepper to taste

Here's what you do:

1 Slice up your tomatoes and peach into thin to medium wedges and add gently to mixing bowl. If there's any juice on the cutting board—and there should be—dump it into the mixing bowl along with the slices.

2 Slice the cheese into thin slices as well and add to bowl.

3 Rough-chop the basil and add to bowl.

4 Now add splashes of olive oil and vinegar. By all means, you can measure it out—should be about a capful of oil and 2 capfuls of vinegar—or you can just drizzle it all over. As long as you don't add a *ton*, you can't mess this up.

5 Now gently stir everything together, being sure not to bruise the peaches or mash anything. Gently pour into serving bowl or plate. Add salt and pepper to taste.

WATERMELON FETA KICK SALAD

DIFFICULTY: Easy • **MAKES:** 4 servings

This dish screams summer to me. It's sweet and a little bit spicy. It has the weird soft-crunchiness of watermelon and the gooey bite of tangy cheese. But best of all, this is a dish your children can whip up while you're working on something else. We like to serve this for guests because of the "wow factor." They always eat it and say, "Wow!"

Here's what you need:

TOOLS

❑ Knife, cutting board, large mixing bowl, measuring cup

INGREDIENTS

❑ 1 small watermelon, or 5 precut wedges if that's what you can find

❑ ¼ cup feta cheese

❑ 1 sprig mint

❑ Small pinch of red chili flakes

Here's what you do:

1 Slice your watermelon into bite-sized chunks and add to mixing bowl.

2 Crumble your feta into little chunks and add to mixing bowl. Big, small, make a mix. Doesn't have to be perfect.

3 Rough-chop the mint and add to bowl.

4 Now, the final part is the tough part. Some kids like spice. Others don't. Some adults do and don't as well. When you make this the first time, just add the smallest pinch of red pepper flakes you're comfortable with. You don't want to overpower this dish and turn it into a hotbed of pain. You want to add just the teeniest hint of heat that will leave people wondering if they're imagining things or if, in fact, your fresh salad has a little kick to it. You can always just skip this part, but it's also a good introduction to the wonders of spice for kids who might otherwise not try it.

CARNY BAKED POTATO CHIPS

DIFFICULTY: Easy-medium • **MAKES:** 1 potato

This fun recipe is straight out of some wild county fair. On one hand, you have a wonderful baked potato that's soft and creamy deep inside. On the other hand, you have these crispy baked potato chips on top that are redolent of garlic and salt and oil. It's a great flavor and texture combination that makes an unexpected weeknight surprise.

Here's what you need:

TOOLS

❏ Oven, oven mitts, knife, cutting board, cookie sheet

INGREDIENTS

❏ 1 large potato

❏ 1 tablespoon olive oil

❏ Salt and pepper

❏ 3–4 cloves garlic

❏ ¼ cup grated Cheddar cheese (optional, but come on, why not?)

Here's what you do:

1 Preheat oven to 350°F.

2 This one is all in the prep. Wash your potato and set on cutting board. You're going to slice partway through the potato. Have your helper take a good chef's knife and make slices from end to end. Imagine you're cutting the potato up into thin chips. Only instead of cutting all the way through to make circular chips, cut only halfway through the potato. The top should have slices all the way from end to end, while the bottom is perfectly intact.

3 Now, rub with olive oil all over and sprinkle with salt and pepper.

4 Peel and smash garlic cloves and then try your best to fit some garlic between slices. Some slices are easy to separate, while others are tough. Do your best. Doesn't have to be perfect.

5 When your potato is ready to go, put it on a cookie sheet, pop into oven, and cook for about 50 minutes or so. When you think it's ready—poke bottom with knife to test; knife should go in easy—remove from oven briefly and sprinkle on cheese. Cook for another couple of minutes, or until cheese is melted. Remove and let cool a tiny bit to eat with hands.

SWEET GINGER CARROTS

DIFFICULTY: Medium • **MAKES:** 4–6 servings

Carrots are already among my favorite foods. It's really hard to mess them up. Take them right out of the fridge and they're a raw, crunchy snack. Bake them, steam them, boil them, you name it, and they're sweet and soft and just oh so right. I like that this recipe makes them soft and crispy at the same time, while also making them sweet and incredibly savory. This side dish is a perfect complement to heavier fare and requires pretty good timing, so it's a nice one for intermediate sous chefs.

Here's what you need:

TOOLS

❏ Stove, frying pan, large lid, knife, cutting board, grater or microplane, measuring cups and spoons, spoon, spatula

INGREDIENTS

❏ 1 pound whole carrots

❏ Fresh ginger, to grate into 1 tablespoon

❏ 2 tablespoons brown sugar

❏ 2 tablespoons butter

❏ ¼ cup water

❏ 1 tablespoon olive oil

❏ ½ teaspoon coarse salt

Here's what you do:

1 First things first: Let's prep. Wash and slice your carrots into circles. Try to make them as uniform as possible, so they cook at the same rate.

2 Now grate your ginger into a nice little pile. If you use a microplane, it should be pasty. Measure out your brown sugar, butter, and water.

3 Heat your frying pan to high and add a splash of olive oil. Now add the carrots, then the water.

4 Bring the water to a simmering boil, then top with lid and lower temperature to low. Cook for about 10 minutes, or until the carrots are soft. You want to steam/boil the carrots basically until they're cooked and the water burns off. And then the fun begins.

5 When the carrots are cooked through but not falling apart (about 10 minutes), remove lid and add butter, ginger, sugar, and a dash of the salt. Turn heat to medium-high.

6 You're going to want to cook off excess water and liquid. Stir around from time to time to make sure the carrots don't burn, but you also want them to take on a nice crispiness. Don't be afraid of a little browning or blackening, but stir to prevent overcooking.

7 Keep this up for about 4–5 minutes. The liquid should be gone, leaving behind perfectly caramelized carrots that are redolent of ginger and butter and sweetness. Sprinkle with a dash more salt before serving.

GREEN BEANS WITH ALMONDS

DIFFICULTY: Medium • **MAKES:** 4–6 servings

Green beans are relatively easy to find at a farmers' market—or perhaps even in your own backyard if you have a green thumb. If so, let kids harvest them just for this dish. By the end of the meal, we always abandon our forks and just dig in with our fingers—like eating a healthier version of French fries.

Here's what you need:

TOOLS

❑ Large frying pan, lid, pot holders, knife, cutting board, strainer, measuring cups and spoons

INGREDIENTS

❑ ½ pound fresh green beans

❑ 1 tablespoon olive oil

❑ ¼ cup water

❑ 1 tablespoon butter

❑ ¼ cup slivered almonds

❑ Salt and pepper dashes

Here's what you do:

1 Trim off the ends of each green bean and toss the finished beans into your strainer. Rinse them when you're done trimming.

2 Now toss them into your large frying pan with olive oil and crank up the heat to high.

Don't worry about butter yet. Just get everything on the road to hot.

3 After about a minute, gently pour in the water, being careful of splashes. Bring to a simmering boil, then lower heat to low and cover with lid. Cook for about 5 minutes.

4 Remove lid and strain excess water into sink. The beans should be cooked at this point but still crisp, not limp.

5 Now the tasty part. Bring heat back up to medium-high and dump in your butter, almonds, and some good dashes of salt and pepper. Stir around occasionally and let everything marinate. Don't be afraid of a little char. But also don't let them burn too much.

6 After about 4 minutes or so, remove from heat and get ready to dig in.

DESSERTS

7

Much to the displeasure of our own little sous chef, we're not an everyday dessert family. But when we do make desserts, we tend to go all out.

Cookies in coffee mugs. Edible mud pies. Mini DIY trifles. Cupcakes baked *inside* eggshells.

Dessert can be, indeed, something special.

I tried to include a few different things that could be used either as meal finishers or as sure-fire party favorites. All of these desserts can be made by a burgeoning chef on her own, or with a little tag-team help from you. At their heart, they're all a little zany and playful—something to really please the palate and tickle a few funny bones along the way. Plus, there's a fantastic banana bread recipe from one of my favorite dads out there.

So get ready to have some serious fun in the kitchen and top off any meal with one last, sweet bite.

DIY MINI-TRIFLE

DIFFICULTY: Easy • **MAKES:** 1 serving

I love DIY trifles not just because they're easy and delicious, but because you can add so much fruit that they become a colorful bonanza of goodness. Kids like to make these all by themselves because it's as easy as slicing and dicing and then stacking everything together. So sit back after dinner and let your little chef whip up something fabulous for dessert. This is a wonderful starter dessert since it's no-bake.

Here's what you need:

TOOLS
❑ Parfait glass (a tall drinking glass will do fine), spoon, knife, cutting board, measuring cups

INGREDIENTS
❑ 1 slice pound cake

❑ ½ cup whipped cream

❑ 4 strawberries

❑ ½ cup blueberries

❑ Granola (for an optional crunchy top)

Here's what you do:

1. Slice the pound cake into cubes. That's seriously the hard part.

2. Now start to fill your glass with alternating ingredients. Add a layer of some cake, and then some fruit, and then some whipped cream, and then repeat the whole layering process all the way up the glass.

3. Keep a little whipped cream for the top. Sprinkle on some granola for crunch to finish it off, or not. Up to your chef.

FIVE-MINUTE CHOCOLATE CHIP MUG COOKIES

DIFFICULTY: Easy • **MAKES:** 1 mug cookie

Virtually everyone loves a warm chocolate chip cookie. But hauling out the electric mixer, cleaning messy bowls, and dealing with baking sheet after baking sheet of individually shaped cookies? I can do without that part. Hence this miracle: The chocolate chip cookie made in a coffee mug and cooked in the microwave. Even the youngest kids can do it by themselves, as it doesn't require any mixers or hot ovens. You just need a mug, a fork, a microwave, and regular cookie-making ingredients. Add a dollop of ice cream to the finished product and you have a sweet hit that is just right for a small dessert for a bunch of kids at a sleepover—or even a TV-time snack after your little sous chefs go to bed. Yum. Any way you serve it, this is sure to be an awesome hit for the whole family.

Here's what you need:

TOOLS

❏ Microwave, coffee mug, measuring spoons, spoon or fork

INGREDIENTS

❏ 1 tablespoon butter, melted

❏ 1 tablespoon white sugar

❏ 1 tablespoon packed brown sugar

❏ Pinch salt (I like Maldon or kosher because you can feel it)

❏ 1 egg yolk

❏ Cap of pure vanilla extract

❏ 3–4ish tablespoons all-purpose flour

❏ 2 tablespoons chocolate chips

❏ Ice cream (optional, but don't be foolish: Go for it.)

Here's what you do:

1 Melt butter in your mug in the microwave.

2 Have your sous chef add sugars and your salt to the butter and stir.

3 Now add your egg yolk and vanilla and stir some more. You should be in smell heaven right about now.

4 Flour. This is a source of constant debate and upheaval in our house. I say just about nearly 4 tablespoons, while my wife prefers a little less. So add in somewhere between 3 and 4 tablespoons of flour and stir it around until you think it resembles cookie dough. I like my cookie slightly denser, so I always add close to 4. My wife prefers less tasty cookies, so she uses less. But no less than 3 tablespoons. We're agreed on that. Feel free to tinker a few times to get it right for your tastes. I know. Tough work. (But seriously, just shy of 4 tablespoons is the best.)

5 Now add your chocolate chips and stir. Use as many as you like or as little as you like. (If it's late and I want a herd of girls to go to bed sometime in the near future, I only let them use, say, a tablespoon of chips, and it works just fine.)

6 Now, microwave. I recommend 45 seconds. My wife recommends 40 seconds. Again, household debate. The cookie will appear almost wet and sheeny after 45 seconds and you'll think it's not done. But it is.

7 So now you have a cookie in a mug and very little mess to clean up. If you'd like, add a couple of dollops of ice cream and enjoy front row seats to the crazy delicious show.

PINEAPPLE UPSIDE-DOWN PANCAKES

DIFFICULTY: Medium • **MAKES:** 16 pancakes

Make pancakes for breakfast and you're a hero. Sometimes it's really that simple. But add yummy stuff to them and suddenly you're a superhero. Because let's face it, stuff in pancakes rocks. And if you think breakfast for dinner is a hit, wait till you try this breakfast for *dessert*. This pineapple upside-down pancake is a griddle-cake take on the traditional favorite. It's sweet, caramelly, pancake-y, and perfect to turn an ordinary breakfast staple into a great after-dinner mini-cake that even the youngest child can help with.

Here's what you need:

TOOLS

❑ Stove, griddle pan, measuring cups and spoons, spoon, large bowl, small bowl, whisk, knife, cutting board, round cookie cutter or solid shot glass, spatula

INGREDIENTS

❑ 1 cup all-purpose flour

❑ 1 tablespoon white sugar

❑ 1 tablespoon brown sugar, plus more for sprinkling

❑ 1 teaspoon baking powder

❑ 1 cup milk

❑ 1 egg, lightly beaten

❑ 1 pineapple (or precut circular slices)

❑ 2 tablespoons butter

Here's what you do:

1 Let's start with the batter. In a large bowl, mix all your dry ingredients. In a small bowl, mix all your wet ingredients—the milk and egg.

2 Now pour the wet over the dry and whisk together until smooth—no lumps.

3 Now you're ready for the pineapple. Buy one that smells like pineapple. As in, it should be fragrant. To prepare, slice off the beautiful top and then slice off the bottom so you have a nice base. Now, slice off the rough sides from top to bottom, taking about ¼" or so with each slice. Remove any brown "eyes." Now here's the fun part. Flip the pineapple on its side and slice thin circles about ⅛" or so each. Don't worry if you can't get 16. Make as many thin circles as you can. When you have a whole bunch of circles, put one down on a cutting board and use a round cookie cutter or a strong shot glass and put it over the core. Press down and remove core. This gets rid of the hard inner core and makes a perfect pineapple circle ready for eating.

4 So now you have all your ingredients prepared and you're ready to cook. Melt a tablespoon of butter on a grill pan, using the spatula to coat everywhere.

5 Put about 4 pineapple slices down, or as many as you can fit. Sprinkle tops with brown sugar, grill for about 45 seconds, then flip.

6 Once you flip, pour batter over each pineapple circle and cook until dough begins to bubble and the edges appear golden brown. Flip at that point and cook for an additional minute. Drizzle your delicious pineapple pancakes with maple syrup or serve as is. They should be sugary and grilled-tasting—a perfect combination.

ICE CREAM MUD PIE

DIFFICULTY: Easy • **MAKES:** 1 pie

Kiddos go nuts for these ice cream mud pies with worms and dirt and backyard happiness, and you'll be thinking: "Seriously, you just smashed up cookies and put it on top of ice cream? Is it really *that* cool?" Well . . . yes, yes it is. This is another great sleepover hit that the kiddos can prepare all on their own and have an absolute blast doing it.

Here's what you need:

TOOLS

❏ Small bowls, ice cream scoop, plastic baggies

INGREDIENTS

❏ 2 Oreo cookies

❏ ¼ cup ice cream of choice

❏ A couple of gummy worms

Here's what you do:

1. First, put the cookies in a bag and mash them up into "dirt." Yes, of course, you can take out the cream first, but I don't know what kind of monster would do that.

2. Layer bottom of bowl with ice cream. Now cover ice cream with your cookie dirt. Insert a few worms into the scene to (a) make it look like a natural mud pie and (b) induce a sure sugar coma. Sorry about that. But isn't that what sleepovers are all about?

EGGSHELL CUPCAKES

DIFFICULTY: Hard • **MAKES:** 1 dozen eggshell cupcakes

Emme and I tinkered with this one for a long, long time until we got it just right. It started with brownies inside eggshells, and then cake, and then soon it morphed into a magical recipe in which you remove the egg insides and replace it with cake and frosting "yolk." It became such a sure-fire hit that we included it in our craft book, *Dad's Book of Awesome Projects*. I'm reproducing it here because it's a great way to get dirty in the kitchen, tinker together, and make something that will knock anyone's socks off.

Here's what you need:

TOOLS

❑ Oven, muffin pan, oven mitts, knife, bowls, tinfoil, plastic sandwich bag, toothpicks, baking syringe (another sandwich bag will also work if you can't find a syringe)

INGREDIENTS

❑ 1 box yellow cake mix (for this, you'll probably also need an egg or 2 and some water and oil)

❑ 12 eggs

❑ 1 tub yellow or white frosting (either buy yellow frosting or dye the white)

❑ Yellow food coloring, if needed

❑ Vegetable oil or oil spray

❑ Egg dye and crayons for decoration (optional)

Here's what you do:

1 Have your sous chef prepare the cake batter according to package directions, while you preheat the oven to 350°F.

2 While your kitchen helper makes the cake batter, prepare the eggs. It's easy. Simply punch a hole in the bottom with a knife point or anything sharp and punchy and then use your fingers to open up a quarter-sized hole. Save the egg innards in a bowl and rinse out the shells. Some eggs can be used for the cake mix, and the rest can be used for dinner. (I like to do this project in the afternoon or very early in the morning, because there's a lot of leftover eggs for an omelet or a dinner frittata or whatever you like.)

3 When the eggs are all hollowed out, prepare the muffin pan by making little nests out of tinfoil. They don't have to be perfect and there's no correct way to do it—just make sure the eggs can stand up straight for baking and you're good to go.

4 Now, spray the inside of the eggs with oil and swirl it around to coat. This is key to preventing sticking when you're later peeling the eggs to get at the cupcakes. Shake out any excess oil.

5 Pour some cake batter into a sandwich bag to make your own pastry bag. Cut a hole in the corner of the bag and then squeeze the batter into the egg holes. Fill them absolutely no more than ¾ full or they will ooze during baking. (They'll probably ooze anyway, but you can cut down on this by filling just above halfway.)

6 Bake away. Try 15 minutes at first and then test them with a toothpick. The toothpick should come out clean. If not, bake a little longer until ready.

7 Now, the fun part. When the eggs are done and cooled a little bit, break out your frosting.

8 It's syringe time! This part is so much fun. You can usually get syringes at an art supply store or a kitchenware store. Stuff the syringe with frosting and then poke it through the egg hole and into the cake. Fill the cake eggs with as much as you think they'll hold without bursting. If you can't find a syringe, no worries. Prepare your frosting and add to another sandwich bag just like you did with the batter. Cut off tip of sandwich bag and do your best to insert tip into cooked cake batter and squeeze. I've found it does the trick just fine.

9 Clean off any excess cake ooze. No matter what you do, the cake may ooze out of the egg. No big deal. Use a sharp knife to scrape the ooze away and then a wet paper towel to clean it all off. Voila! Your eggs are ready to go. Enjoy the coolest-looking cupcake you will ever eat in your life.

DAD TIP

You can dye the eggs beforehand for special events. Or you can simply use crayons to decorate them when you're done baking. We like to serve the eggs in their carton, because they look raw and uncooked. Take a few out and enjoy the surprised looks you get.

GRAHAM CRACKER HOUSES

DIFFICULTY: Easy • **MAKES:** 1 house

Long before we got married and had a child, Dana and I decided during the holidays that we were going to manufacture a gingerbread house from scratch. There's a reason we have never repeated this task. It. was. hard. First, you have to make the dough and then the house pieces, an engineering feat we couldn't quite accomplish with the tools we had on hand. Then we made all the frosting and fudges and candies we wanted to make. I think we abandoned the project after 2 days or so. It was such a burden that the project almost turned me off to cracker houses forever. Almost. But then I discovered these graham cracker houses. They are *easy* and actually perfect for any time of the year and any style building—or vehicle. Castles, houses, airplanes, you name it, kids can build it. With a lot less stress.

Here's what you need:

TOOLS

❏ Spoons, flat surface for making, butter knives for shaping

INGREDIENTS

❏ 4 or more whole graham cracker rectangles

❏ ½ cup peanut butter

❏ Bunch o' tubes of cake-decorating icing

❏ Candies of choice: gumdrops, kisses, M&M's, sprinkles, whatever you like

Here's what you do:

1 There's not much in the way of instructions, other than you're going to use the crackers as your walls and roof, and the peanut butter as your glue. You can make pretty much anything you want.

2 But for the sake of instructions, let's build a house. Break off a piece of cracker—the rectangles usually make 2 squares—and put 1 square on decorating surface.

3 Spoon peanut butter along sides of cracker and then add 4 walls. Use your fingers to apply peanut butter along wall corners to hold everything in place.

4 I like to make a flat roof by simply laying a cracker on top of everything. But give it a solid mid-century vibe by first putting candies atop the edge of one wall. When you then place a cracker on as a roof, it tilts. It's a cool touch that's more structurally sound than an A-frame design.

5 Now decorate until your heart's content. Add layer of peanut butter to the roof and top with candies. Do the same on any walls you like. Use the icing tubes to add doors and windows. Don't be surprised if you want to make your own alongside the kids.

WACKY CAKE

DIFFICULTY: Easy • **MAKES:** 1 cake

My friend and fellow stay-at-home dad, Graham, shared this recipe with me years ago, and it's always been a favorite. It's a no-nonsense, messy experience that lets kids take the lead and get their fingers and hands dirty. It ain't the fanciest gourmet cake you'll ever find. But man, kids dig it. Younger kids can do just about every step, and older kids can complete it all on their own. Thanks, Graham.

Here's what you need:

TOOLS

❏ Oven, 8" × 8" cake pan, oven mitts, whisk or spoon, measuring cups and spoons

INGREDIENTS

❏ 1 tablespoon butter

❏ 1½ cup all-purpose flour

❏ 1 cup sugar

❏ ½ teaspoon salt

❏ 3 tablespoons cocoa powder

❏ 1 teaspoon baking soda

❏ 1 teaspoon white vinegar

❏ 2 teaspoons pure vanilla extract

❏ 6 tablespoons vegetable oil

❏ 1 cup water

❏ Powdered sugar (optional)

❏ Ice cream (why not?)

Here's what you do:

1 Preheat the oven to 350°F. Grease sides and bottom of pan with butter.

2 Whisk dry ingredients together in a bowl. Again, let your helper take the lead. But it's a great starter recipe for baking for kids.

3 Now here's the cool and messy part, and also the reason I've seen this recipe called Hole Cake. Once the dry ingredients are ready, have your sous chef make 3 holes in the mixture.

4 In one hole, pour the vinegar. In the second hole, add the vanilla. Add oil to the third.

5 Now pour your water over the whole thing and whisk around until smooth.

6 Pour batter into greased cake pan and cook for 35 or so minutes, or until a knife inserted into cake comes out clean. Sprinkle with powdered sugar to decorate or add some ice cream on the side.

BACON CHIP COOKIES

DIFFICULTY: Medium • **MAKES:** 2 dozen cookies

So what's better than coming home to a house smelling like fresh-baked cookies? Coming home to a house that smells like cookies and *bacon*. Yum. This is a recipe that took us a while to get right, but it was certainly fun to eat all the experiments. Now, we top half the cookies with bacon and leave the other half as is, or even sometimes top with coarse Maldon salt. We ultimately decided to make a nice go-to chocolate chip cookie recipe that tastes great on its own. But it can also be modified toward the end of baking to include bacon chips for the pork lover in your life. You'll also notice that there is no precise measurement for chocolate chips. I like to measure these by kid handfuls because it's fun, and it's also pretty easy to tell when you have enough. So get ready to make the best cookies ever.

Here's what you need:

TOOLS

❏ Oven, cooling rack, cookie sheets, oven mitts, measuring cups and spoons, mixing spoon, mixer, 2 mixing bowls, whisk

INGREDIENTS

❏ 2 strips of bacon

❏ ½ cup white sugar

❏ ½ cup packed brown sugar

❏ 1 egg

❏ 1 stick butter, room temperature

❏ 1 pinch salt

❏ 2 capfuls pure vanilla extract

❏ 1¼ cup all-purpose flour

❏ ½ teaspoon baking powder

❏ 4 kid-sized handfuls chocolate chips

❏ ¼ tablespoon butter (for greasing sheets)

❏ 1 big pinch Maldon salt

Here's what you do:

1 Preheat the oven to 375°F. Place bacon on cooling rack and then put cooling rack on one of your cookie sheets. Bake bacon for 15 or so minutes or until crispy. You don't need a cooling rack, but it helps drain fat from the bacon while cooking. Just make sure your bacon is crispy, OK?

2 While the bacon is cooking, get your dough ready. In a large mixing bowl, beat together the sugars, egg, butter, salt, and vanilla.

3 Have your sous chef whisk together flour and baking powder in another bowl.

4 When sugar-egg mixture is smooth, slowly add flour mixture to mixing bowl, mixing, say, half at a time to make your dough.

5 Add chocolate chips to dough and mix until chips are well distributed.

6 Remove bacon from oven and let cool, while you spread cookie dough in tablespoon-sized drops on other greased cookie sheets. Now, lots of recipes say you're going to get up to 3 dozen or more cookies from simple chocolate chip cookie dough. But I've never seen it happen. We usually get 1 to 2 dozen, as we like big cookies. Just bake longer if you have slightly bigger cookies.

7 Speaking of which . . . bake for about 10 minutes. They should be brown on edges. The longer you bake them, the crispier they become.

8 While cookies are baking, remove all fat from bacon. Chop only the crispy meat parts into bitty chips. When your cookies are about 2 minutes from being finished, quickly open oven and pull out sheet. Sprinkle bacon on top of as many cookies as you want. Then finish cooking. (I know what you're thinking: Why not just top cookies before putting in oven? Well, the bacon fat somehow tinkers with everything and makes the cookies wrinkly and weird looking. I've found that topping with just minutes to go crisps the bacon without messing up the cookie.)

9 When done, remove cookies and let cool. On cookies that are not topped with bacon, you can sprinkle a small pinch of coarse salt on top for a super tasty treat. Or just leave as is. Either way you do this, you're going to be a kitchen superhero and your sous chefs will be stoked to make something so tasty and special. Serve with milk. *Aww yah.*

RAINBOW CUPCAKES

DIFFICULTY: Medium • **MAKES:** 2 dozen cupcakes

OK, I cheat on this one. Bigtime. I don't have a favorite cake recipe, so I usually just grab an off-the-shelf cupcake mix from the store for this. It's a relatively easy recipe to begin with, but the store-bought mix makes it even easier. You make the mix, divide it up into bowls, dye everything with different colors, and then splash everything into a muffin pan. Easy. Fun. And oh my gosh, if you ever make these without the kiddos, just wait until you see their faces when they take a bite. This is perfect for a surprise party or for cooking with a kid wanting to make a fun classroom birthday treat.

Here's what you need:

TOOLS

❏ Oven, several cupcake pans, oven mitts, cupcake liners, measuring cups and spoons, 1 large mixing bowl, 4 small mixing bowls, lots of stirring implements

INGREDIENTS

❏ 1 box of vanilla or white cupcake mix (for this, you'll probably also need an egg or 2 and some water and oil)

❏ 1 tub of white frosting (See? Cheater.)

❏ Food coloring (Nope, there is nothing healthy about this one. Yum!)

❏ Sprinkles or decorations (optional)

Here's what you do:

1 Preheat the oven to what the box says, usually 350°F.

2 Now prepare the mix according to box directions—stir up the mix with an egg or 2, some water, and some oil. Kids can usually do all this solo. Let 'em.

3 You should have a big ol' bowl of white batter. Divide it among your 4 smaller mixing bowls. Add 1 color of dye to each bowl. Stir until each bowl is well mixed.

4 I like to use dark cupcake liners so the surprise of a rainbow cupcake underneath isn't ruined until kids peel and eat. Add a spoonful of batter to a liner. Now dump in another spoonful from a different bowl of color. Don't mix. Just spoon in and leave. It sort of oozes around and that's fine. Keep dumping in new spoonfuls of color in each liner until ¾ full.

5 Bake according to box—20ish minutes—and then pull out to cool on a rack. Let cool before you top with frosting. Decorate the tops with sprinkles. Serve and watch the joy.

EDIBLE FINGERPAINT

DIFFICULTY: Easy • **MAKES:** 2 cups of paint

I have yet to find a kid who doesn't like to fingerpaint. (Just as I have yet to find a parent who enjoys cleaning it all up, so apologies in advance; this one is super messy. But the joy is worth it.) Some kids try to eat paint anyway—but with this recipe, you can relax and not worry about . . . the fact that your kid eats paint.

Here's what you need:

TOOLS
❑ Mixing bowl, measuring cup, whisk, muffin pan, spoons, wax paper

INGREDIENTS
❑ 1 (4-ounce) packet of instant vanilla pudding

❑ 2 cups cold water

❑ Food coloring

Here's what you do:

1 In the mixing bowl, whisk the pudding with the water until it's, well, pudding.

2 Now pour the pudding into the muffin pan. Each little cup will be its own color, so use as many little cups as you have colors for.

3 Now stir several drops of food coloring into the cups to make separate colors.

4 Put in the fridge to chill out for 10–15 minutes.

5 While it's cooling, prepare your work surface. I like to use wax paper. You can paint on it and then lick straight off of it. If you have those chip bag clippy thingies, you can clamp the wax paper down on a table. Otherwise, you can use light weights, like spoons, to keep the corners down. Of course, you can use other items as your canvas as well: plates, cookie sheets, walls. (Kidding.) Just make sure that if more than one kid is painting, you have separate muffin pans and canvases for each, otherwise you're going to have a germ factory of the highest order.

ANYTHING CRUMBLE

DIFFICULTY: Medium • **MAKES:** 6 servings

Full disclosure: For the longest time, I refused to eat cooked fruit. My mother-in-law would make these delicious crumbles and cobblers, and I'd pick away at the crunchy, sweet topping but leave the fruit behind as if she were trying to poison me. (Which, for the record, was entirely possible. I'm on to you, Marilyn.) On a trip to France, I was forced by an incredible bout of hangry to dive into a hand-held apple pie. "Do they always taste like this?" I marveled. In a bite, I was sold. Now whenever I head to the in-laws', I can't wait for the cobblers and crumbles—the crunchy tops made even better by the addition of warm fruit and cold ice cream. Turns out, they're relatively easy to make, and I've been eating them ever since.

Here's what you need:

TOOLS
- ❑ Oven, 8" × 8" baking pan or dish, oven mitts, peeler, knife, cutting board, mixing bowls, measuring cups and spoons, big spoons for stirring

INGREDIENTS
- ❑ 3 large apples (I like Granny Smith)
- ❑ 4 tablespoons brown sugar, divided
- ❑ 4 tablespoons all-purpose flour, divided
- ❑ 1 cap pure vanilla extract
- ❑ 2 teaspoons cinnamon, divided
- ❑ 2 pinches salt, divided
- ❑ 2 tablespoons butter, melted
- ❑ ¾ cup quick-cooking oats

Here's what you do:

1 Preheat the oven to 400°F.

2 Peel and then dice up the apples into bite-sized chunks. Work as a team here, as one chops and the other assembles the ingredients to make the filling and the topping.

3 Throw all your apples into a mixing bowl, then add 2 tablespoons brown sugar, 2 tablespoons flour, vanilla, 1 teaspoon cinnamon, and 1 pinch of salt. Stir and let sit while you move on to the next step.

4 Now it's time for the topping. In another mixing bowl, combine 2 tablespoons brown sugar, 2 tablespoons flour, the butter, the oats, 1 teaspoon cinnamon, and 1 pinch salt. Stir until everything is well mixed.

5 Now toss your apples into your baking pan. Spread the crumble mixture evenly over the top.

6 Bake for 45 minutes or until fruit is soft and the top is crumbly, golden brown. Here's a tip: If you think the top is cooking too fast and browning too much, cover with tinfoil about halfway through. You still get the golden brown, but it won't darken any more.

7 We like to serve this with the creamiest, richest vanilla ice cream you can find. Just scoop out a bunch of the crumble and toss it into a bowl and top with ice cream. I seriously can't believe I avoided this dessert for so long. Foolish. Foolish, I tell ya.

DAD TIP

By all means, tinker around with other fruit. Peaches and plums are perfect for a summer crumble. I like apples in the fall. Berries make great late-summer crumbles. Have fun with it.

THE ROCKY FUDGE ROAD

DIFFICULTY: Medium • **MAKES:** 2 dozen squares

If anything reminds me of childhood on a plate, it's this. It always brings me back to Mackinac Island in northern Michigan—a resort town where there are no cars and tons of fudge. It's a special place, and I'll always remember walking into a candy shop where they made fudge in front of all the customers. They'd tempt you with samples and all of a sudden you're headed home with tiny boxes laden with fudge-y goodness. Every time we make this, I'm brought back to that time and can just taste the magic of the butter-smelling shops and the tiny boxes of magic, just waiting to be opened.

Here's what you need:

TOOLS

❏ Stove, large saucepan, rimmed cookie sheet, measuring cups and spoons, stirring spoons

INGREDIENTS

❏ 3 cups sugar

❏ 1½ sticks butter

❏ ⅔ cup evaporated milk

❏ 1 (12-ounce) bag of chocolate chips

❏ 1 (7-ounce) jar of marshmallow cream

❏ 1 cap pure vanilla extract

❏ ¼ cup chopped walnuts

❏ ¼ cup crushed pretzels

❏ ¼ cup small marshmallows

❏ Cooking spray

Here's what you do:

1 In a large saucepan, combine sugar, butter, and milk, and stir constantly over medium heat until it all melts and boils (probably 5 minutes).

2 Turn off the heat and remove the pan from the burner, then quickly add chocolate chips and stir until they melt.

3 Next, add the marshmallow cream and the cap of vanilla and stir until good and mixed.

4 Spray your rimmed cookie sheet with cooking spray (any big pan with sides will do) and pour in fudge mixture. Make a nice layer all over.

5 Here's where personal preference comes into play. You *can* just throw the cookie sheet into the fridge as is and wait for it to harden (4 hours), or you can be a responsible human being and top your fudge mixture with nuts and pretzels and miniature marshmallows. I usually add the marshmallows right away and then throw the fudge in the fridge for an hour before sprinkling on the nuts and pretzels. The marshmallows get absorbed a little this way, while the other bits stay crunchy. But again, by all means, let your kid decide what to do.

6 Once your creation is topped appropriately, let everything chill for about 4 hours before biting into a dessert I hope brings you back to the joys of your own childhood.

BOOMIN' BANANA BREAD

Contributed by Doyin Richards

DIFFICULTY: Easy • **MAKES:** 12 servings

I've been following Doyin Richards online for a long time now. He's the fabulous founder of the site Daddy Doin' Work (*www.daddydoinwork.com*)—you seriously need to "like" it on Facebook for more—and author of the book, *Daddy Doin' Work: Empowering Mothers to Evolve Fatherhood.* He's a strong advocate for involved fatherhood and, frankly, he is just a nice dude. Thankfully for us, he's also an incredible chef with a like-minded philosophy when it comes to getting kids involved in cooking. Here's Doyin on working with kids and making fabulous meals together:

Sure, playing at the park with the kids is fun—but what's better than baking in the kitchen? For the life of me, I'll never understand men who despise cooking. Generally speaking, men like to build things, right? Well, what's better than building something that you can eat afterwards? I'm going out on a limb by saying that eating a desk chair or a coffee table probably isn't too satisfying. Baking is fun for the kids because they learn about measurements, counting, using the proper ingredients, temperatures, and most importantly—patience. They can eat some of the batter, but not all of it.

The Boomin' Banana Bread recipe is a favorite because it's so incredibly easy to make, and my oldest daughter loves to mash the bananas. It's a tasty treat that can be added to a kid's lunchbox but it's also sweet enough for an after-dinner treat. Very few breads are so versatile that you enjoy them during any time of the day, but this one does the trick. The best part is that the kids have ownership over it because they helped to make it. And what's better than creating future bakers? Fair warning: the batter is really tasty, so keep an eye on your kids or else your Banana Bread will only be a Banana Slice when it comes out of the oven. Otherwise, enjoy!

Here's what you need:

TOOLS

❑ Oven, square or rectangle baking dish, oven mitts, electric mixer, 3 mixing bowls, measuring cups and spoons, mixing spoons

INGREDIENTS

❑ 1½ cups all-purpose flour

❑ 2 teaspoons baking powder

❑ 1 teaspoon baking soda

❑ ¼ cup vegetable oil

❑ 1 cup sugar

❑ 1 teaspoon pure vanilla extract

❑ 1 egg

❑ 3 ripe bananas

❑ 1 tablespoon butter or cooking spray

❑ ½ cup chopped pecans (optional)

Here's what you do:

1 Preheat the oven to 350°F.

2 In a large mixing bowl, combine flour, baking powder, and baking soda and then set aside.

3 In another mixing bowl, use the electric mixer to beat oil, sugar, vanilla, and egg until light and fluffy.

4 Mash your bananas until, well, mashed. Add them to egg mixture and mix.

5 Now add flour mixture to banana mixture and stir until all ingredients are moistened.

6 Grease baking dish with butter or spray and then pour in batter. Optional: Add chopped pecans to the pan if you like the crunch. Bake for 40 minutes, or until a toothpick inserted into center comes out clean.

7 Let cool for about 10 minutes before serving.

INDEX